REMOVING
THE
HABIT OF GOD

Sister Christine's Story 1959-1968

To Elsa
all the best
Susan
2019

Susan Bassler Pickford

ISBN-10: 188966412x
ISBN-13: 9781889664125
Library of Congress Control Number: 2012906027
S B P Collaboration Works
Portland, Maine

DEDICATED TO

The wonderful women in my life
family, friends, religious
to
the Franciscan Sisters of Millvale, Pennsylvania
the Sisters of Charity of St. Elizabeth, Convent Station, New Jersey
the Sisters of Mercy of Plainfield, New Jersey
the Ursuline Sisters of Tildonk, Long Island, New York

Forsythia
You mock me
Flaunting hope in each lacy golden bough
Forgetting winter's barrenness
Unmindful of the summer's heat
Present glory of yellowness
You live in the Now!

The author

For me removing the habit wasn't as dramatic as it was for Audrey Hepburn in *The Nun's Story*. About a month before I was actually going to leave the convent, I went home for a visit. My mother and I walked into a department store at the local mall. We chose a couple of dresses. I went inside the dressing room and took off my distinctive veil, black dress and dickey and hung them on a hook. Then I chose a rather plain blue dress and pulled it over my head. I parted the curtain just a smidgen so my mother could see.

"Okay," she said.

"Let me try that one," and I pointed to a brown checked dress she had in her arm. When I parted the curtain, Mom said, "That's fine too."

I handed the dresses back to my mother and put on the black habit and veil once again. Some hair was allowed to be seen post Vatican Council but I had let mine grow for the Exit and made sure long wisps weren't curling down my neck. When I came out of the dressing room, a former high school classmate of mine just happened to walk by. "Hi," I said casually as if nuns popped out of department store dressing rooms every day. I turned beet red. I felt furtive and sneaky. I continued on to the counter where my mother paid for the dresses.

What I had just done in the privacy of the department store dressing room reminded me of what I had done nine years earlier when I entered the convent as a seventeen year old. Then my parents, brother, and I drove over three hours to the Ursuline Novitiate at Blue Point, Long Island, New York.

I arrived at the large motherhouse wearing a blue check cotton dress. The Novice Mistress took me and seven other girls upstairs to our rooms. Laid out on the bed was my postulant outfit. I put on the black dress with a small cape and fitted the stiff white collar around my neck and snapped cuffs around my wrists. I picked up a small veil for my head and looked around for a mirror to see what I was doing and learned my first lesson - postulants are not to be vain. I opened the door and followed the others down the steps to the garden where my parents and brother were waiting. Dad took lots of pictures as he always did.

Postulant Susan Ann Bassler
Blue Point, NY, September 8, 1959

As I reflect on the young woman I was then, posing in the garden, I have to wonder what was I doing there. At the time, I would have said, I am following God's will. I had all the answers then, as I stared back at the camera with a sweet, Mona Lisa smile. But why would God want me to leave home at seventeen, give up all worldly goods, never have a dime in my pocket, never make another important decision in my life, and forever give up the right to have a boyfriend, a husband, sex, and children? I have no idea.

Of course, I've had half a century to think about it. During that time much in the world has changed. The Roman Catholic Church has changed. The Catholic school system has changed. The convent has changed. I've changed.

But the truth is that the more things change, the more they stay the same. Mother Teresa's Missionaries of Charity founded in 1950 is known world- wide. The order numbers over 4,500. In 1997 four religious women responding to John Paul II's call for a new evangelization founded the Dominican Sisters of Mary. They number more than one hundred, are growing rapidly and were even on *The Oprah Winfrey Show*. Some generous women will always be drawn to idealistic ideas like moths to a flame.

Nuns can be found among Anglicans, Lutherans, Jains, Buddhists and Taoists. In third world countries where life options for intelligent women are few and arranged marriages are the norm, religious life is attractive. But in the United States among both non-believers and various Protestant denominations, religious life in general and celibacy in particular are viewed with suspicion and even considered abnormal. At the very least nuns are considered fair game for comedians. Nuns are different and thus endlessly fascinating. At various times throughout my life, friends, family, new acquaintances, practicing Catholics, lapsed Catholics, atheists and agnostics have all asked me: So why did you become a nun? To attempt an answer to that question I have to start at the beginning.

Sherman and Ethel Kerr Bassler
Butler, Pennsylvania 1935

My mother fell in love with a handsome, curly headed, Lutheran. However, she didn't want to be married in the rectory to a non-Catholic, so she persuaded my dad to convert, which he did. They were married in St. Paul's Roman Catholic Church in Butler, Pennsylvania. He promised to raise their children in the Catholic faith which he also did. So I was baptized Susan Ann at St. Peter's Church and was sent to the Catholic elementary school run by the Franciscan Sisters. I made my First Confession and First Holy Communion in second grade just like all the other Catholic children.

A photo shows me standing in my Grandmother Kerr's back yard, looking at my dad, who is holding the camera. I have the hint of a smile on my face, a veil on my head, and I am dressed in white from head to toe. My white rosary beads hang perfectly from prayerful hands. I am the personification of innocence. When I read biographies of successful people, I am always amazed at how young they were when they knew for sure what they wanted to be, and how certain they were about what they wanted to do with their lives. When I look at this picture, I know I wanted to be holy. I wanted to be a saint. A mere ten years separates this photograph from that seventeen-year-old postulant who had a lot to learn.

First Holy Communion
Butler, Pennsylvania 1949

As a child I was naturally pliant. I wanted to please at all costs. I loved school and I loved Sister. In fact "Sister said" was the eleventh commandment in our house. My mother reinforced this precept by the merest shake of her head or a sharp look; if either my brother or I would

5

begin to voice any annoyance or irritation about what happened at school. Even though Dad had converted to the Holy Roman Catholic faith, we had to make the case for Catholicism daily. The irony of this was that my mother was terrified of the nuns because when she was a little girl, Sr. Bertha slapped her for not paying attention during an arithmetic drill. My Grandmother Kerr marched on down to the school to explain that my mother had recurring ear infections, which resulted in hearing problems, and she wasn't to be hit again. That slap left deeper scars than those on her eardrums, but I had suffered no such trauma.

I have happy memories of my first three years of school. I still remember my teachers' names: Sr. Maureen, Sr. Grace and Sr. Damian. In first grade I was asked to help a fellow student with his lessons. I was chosen to walk in the procession for the May crowning of the Blessed Mother. I was picked to play the part of the stepmother in our production of *Hansel and Gretel*. My report cards show mostly A's and always A's for Effort and Conduct.

May Procession 1949

"You look like a teacher," Sr. Damian said to me prophetically when I came to her third grade class wearing my new eye glasses. I glowed in her attention and my self-consciousness vanished in an instant. My Grandfather Kerr would walk me up to St. Paul's to see the beautiful manger scene in December and to get my throat blessed on the Feast of St.Blaise in February. Because of World War II Grandpa kept working as an engineer on the Baltimore & Ohio Railroad until he was seventy. After he retired he loved to walk my brother and me to the rail yard to see the trains. My Grandmother Kerr taught me how to crochet and cut quilt squares and play the piano. She made bread for the week and fresh cookies for after school snacks. In the summer, my brother and I went to visit Grandmother Bassler who doted on us some more. She taught me how to sew on her treadle machine. Grandma was a Lutheran and she set up play dates with the Pastor's daughter. On sunny days my Grandmother, brother and I went berry picking. But life was not perfect. My mother was intensely unhappy. I would be forty-five before I knew why. My father who had worked for the Pennsylvania State Police, now worked as a radio operator on ships and returned home between stints at sea. These reunions were always exciting for my brother and me because Dad would arrive with a flourish and special gifts.

Susan, Dad, Billy
Butler, Pennsylvania 1949

One time he came back from Basra on the Persian Gulf. He told stories about the *Kasbah* where he had bought the presents. I imagined my dashing father wandering around an exotic open market of twisted lanes and crowded stalls where eager venders were calling out prices and haggling. My father had bought red fezzes with tassels hanging down the side that we promptly donned and posed for a picture. In it my brother is leaning rakishly on one side of my dad who is squatting on one knee, and I am nuzzling close on the other side looking down adoringly at my father. For years the fezzes collected dust on a closet shelf but then disappeared. A beloved silver ring was also lost behind a sink, but I still have a little girl's leather pocket book with a tinted picture of a palm tree and camel on it.

May was the month of the Blessed Mother. There were May crownings and May processions and many rosaries were said. In fact, Sister had a statue of the Blessed Mother that could be taken for an overnight at students' homes. I knew I had to take my turn, but dreaded it all the same. After supper, my parent's bedroom became our sitting room. The evening I had the statue I brought it out and said the magic words: "Sister said." Everyone knelt down, including my convert father, and we prayed the rosary. The awkwardness was tangible. Our Lady never had a return engagement.

During the summer before I made my First Holy Communion, my brother and I made our annual visit to Grandmother Bassler. We attended the English Evangelical Lutheran Church on Sunday mornings with her. This beautiful church had a large stained glass window of the Good Shepherd in the sanctuary. The church had been founded by our great-grandfather Rev. Gottlieb Bassler in 1843. After services, the pastor stood outside and greeted everyone. My Grandmother B proudly showed off her visiting grandchildren. But after I made my First Holy Communion, my brother and I had to walk to St. Gregory's Catholic Church maybe a half-a-mile away. It wasn't that there were great discussions about religious beliefs, but my mother put a stop to our attending the English Lutheran Church. However, I believed at a very young age that someone didn't have to be a Catholic to be saved. It was unthinkable that my beloved Grandmother Bassler wasn't going to heaven with the rest of us. And even if my father was a half-hearted convert and sometimes ate meat on Friday, I didn't believe he was going to hell either. I kept these heretical thoughts to myself.

Outside of school, I had a few good friends, especially Yvonne and Diane. I'd go to their homes, and they'd come to mine. My friend Yvonne lived down the street from my grandmother's house. Her dad cut hair in a room at the side of their house on Brady Street. They didn't have much money, and one Christmas I gave Yvonne one of my dolls. Once, I went to her house after school without telling my mother. It was dark when I got home, and my mother was frantic. Dad gave me my first and only spanking. Diane lived up the street from my grandmother's house. Diane's dad, who owned an Italian restaurant, had set up old booths in their finished basement where we played. One afternoon when her mother was out, we snuck up to the second floor bathroom. I was impressed with all the marble and mirrors. At my house, Grandpa would put on the radio, and Diane and I would dance in the kitchen and pretend we were Shirley Temple. In the fall we'd sit on Diane's brick porch and watch the birds fly off in great numbers. The first one to spy the flock would shout: "That's how many people will be at my wedding," then we'd laugh. Change was in the air. I would soon be the one flying away. In the middle of fourth grade, I left my friends. I left my school. I left my grandparents, and I left Pennsylvania.

———✦✦✦———

My dad stopped going to sea as mysteriously as he began. He took a job working for the U.S. Army Signal Corps Research and Development at Fort Monmouth, New Jersey. So after living almost five years with my Grandmother and Grandfather Kerr, we packed up and moved to the Garden State in January, 1951. We were a family again.

The move affected each of us in different ways. This was post-World War II America. The war had been won and the energy of victory was infectious. My dad, who held a two-year certificate in radio communications and had acquired one hundred hours in the Fundamentals of Electrical Engineering from Pennsylvania State College did not have a college degree. But a good friend, Ralph

Osche, who had already been hired by the rapidly expanding Signal Corps, convinced him to apply and he did. Under dad's name on an old business card it says: Modular Circuit Systems, Electronic Components Research Dept. The Hexagon, Fort Monmouth, New Jersey. When people asked what does your father do? I'd say he was an Electrical Engineer. For most of his career he acted as a liaison between the government and private contractors along the technology belt – Route 128 in Massachusetts. Most of his colleagues had degrees and many were highly qualified German scientists. Dad was bright enough and did the best he could, but he clearly felt anxious about his position. Returning from vacation, he would often joke that he hoped his desk would still be there. He had given up the love and lure of the sea for a 9 to 5 government job.

My mother had attended Pittsburgh Music Institute for three years to study piano but left before she received a teaching certificate. She performed publicly even on the radio. While my dad was courting her, he sent her a telegram after a performance at Gimbals on station WCAE Pittsburgh: *Just fine Ethel Congratulations.* She had a lively bridge club and was an active member of the Tuesday Musical Club. The move to New Jersey, while necessary for the good of her marriage and family, tore her away from every support group she had ever had. She was intelligent, musically talented, sensitive, romantic, very close to her mother and terribly insecure. As a young woman, she had obtained a driver's license but after a minor accident never drove again until she was sixty. She tried getting a job but that too ended dismally. She taught piano lessons when the opportunity arose. After we moved in with her parents, she suffered severe bouts of depression that did not go away when we moved to New Jersey. Most of the time, she was lonely.

My older brother by three and a half years had his own losses. He also had to leave his school, his grandparents, and his three faithful buddies. Moving in January in the middle of the school year was very difficult. In addition he was concerned about his little sister. I remember being totally miserable standing in the cold, waiting for a public bus to go to school as we tried to comfort each other. We knew better than to complain about making new friends and adjusting to new teachers. We knew instinctively not to burden our mother with our problems.

So gradually I turned to Holy Mother Church and the Blessed Mother for solace. Those words began to take on new meaning in my life. My need turned the figurative into the literal. The mother of Jesus could be my mother too. She would listen whenever I needed a sympathetic ear. I began to pray to Our Lady on a regular basis and I set up a shrine to her in my bedroom. Holy Mother Church became more and more important in my life.

———*◦◦◦*———

At my old school whenever a new student came, the sisters made sure they picked a special buddy for them, and they made a big fuss over the newcomer. I was actually looking forward to moving to a new school and having the sister and classmates make a fuss over me. However, my first day at Star of the Sea Grammar School in Long Branch is forever seared into my memory. I walked to the door of the classroom and stood there while every student stared at me as they walked by. For a shy person this was excruciatingly painful. The sister finally arrived, pointed out my desk, and I quickly sat down. There was no special treatment. I was not made to feel welcome. Another new student arrived. When the sister called on Hans, he jumped to his feet and clicked his heels. Everyone stared. He might as well have dropped in from Pluto. Actually he had arrived from Germany with his scientist father. Welcome to fourth grade. The children had already formed tight circles of friends. I found it difficult to penetrate those circles. Eventually, I made a best friend with Emily who had recently lost her father. Her mother ran a boardinghouse that abutted the schoolyard. Emily and I stayed over at each other's homes, kept secret diaries, survived puberty, and giggled together. We went to Mass on First Fridays, and her Irish mom fixed soft-boiled eggs for breakfast before we headed over to school. Emily is still a dear friend.

I didn't like my new school run by the Sisters of Charity of St. Elizabeth, especially after one nun scolded me for my messy desk and continued on to criticize my former teachers by asking: "Is that what they taught you in Pennsylvania?" However, I was pleased when I was asked to help run the school store before classes. Unfortunately, my special status ended quickly when I was falsely accused of stealing from the money box. That really hurt, but true to form I still tried to please. On Saturday mornings I helped my classroom teacher do her sacristy chores. Our Lady Star of the Sea had banks of vigil lights in front of the statues of St. Joseph and the Blessed Mother. When the candles burned to the bottom of the glass, the metal bases had to be pried out and the glasses washed before new candles were put in. Helping sister made me feel special again, but my mother thought I should be home helping her on Saturday mornings. My mother and I rarely saw eye to eye on things.

The large candles cost a dollar, and I could not afford to light them, but I did on occasion light the small ones. One time before my birthday, I knelt in front of the Blessed Mother and lit a candle and prayed. A woman kneeling next to me witnessed my fervor in prayer.

"What are you praying for?" the woman whispered pleasantly but soon shook her head in disapproval when I answered in a small, thin voice, "A bike."

In sixth grade I went on a field trip with other chosen girls to visit the sisters' motherhouse in Convent Station. They were trying to foster vocations among those they discerned were called by God to the religious life. I was a good girl, not boy crazy, and I was generous to help out on Saturday mornings, so I guess they thought I was a natural. It was after this visit that I first began to think about becoming a sister.

My family moved four more times after our initial exodus from Pennsylvania. The military man that had rented his home to us returned sooner than expected, and we had to move out. The next rented home had a chimney fire right before Christmas, and we had to get out immediately. My poor mother had to take the bus downtown to collect us from school, and when dad got home from work we gathered our belongings and moved again. It was pretty exciting getting pulled out of school. That Christmas all our presents smelled of smoke. My mother had given me a book, *The Luistania*, but it smelled like burnt toast, and every time I turned a page I felt like crying. The next home was a small cape. We were there only a few months because it was undergoing renovations during Easter, so we soon packed up and moved to a duplex on Sixth Avenue.

———ᴓᴓᴓ———

In sixth grade I made my Confirmation. I took the name of Bernadette Soubirous who was born in Lourdes, France on January 7, 1844, and saw visions of the Blessed Mother. She was whisked away into a convent where she died as a young woman in 1879 and was declared a saint in 1933. My best friend Emily took the name, Theresa

Confirmation 1953
Sixth Avenue, Long Branch, NJ

Finally, in the middle of seventh grade, my mother found a house we could afford. She said it cost $12,000 but years later confessed she got it for $7,000. So in 1953 we moved permanently to 5 William St., Red Bank, New Jersey. I couldn't bear to start another new school in January, so I rode the public bus from Red Bank to Long Branch every day until June.

It was while we lived in the home with the chimney fire that I remember doing something rather odd. It probably happened after my trip to the motherhouse. I decided to take a "vow of silence" and wore a plaid dishtowel over my head pinned at the nape of my neck. I don't remember how long I played at being a nun and not speaking, but no one paid any attention to me. However, it was in that house that my mother planned a birthday party - my second and last. So perhaps she was concerned. I have little memory of the actual party except that in my eyes it was a total failure. My expectations of being the center of attention didn't materialize. I did not have a good time and I was terribly disappointed in both the effort and the outcome. Forget about being holy, I wanted to be popular.

But I felt I had an image problem. We were a family of readers. I was a bookworm and I wore glasses. I had happy childhood memories of going with my mother to the library. I loved everything about books and libraries. I especially loved the beautiful formal libraries depicted in movies. One time a nun asked me: "Susan, does your family have a library?" I immediately thought of a large room with a standing globe, leather chairs and lamps with dark, green lampshades and floor to ceiling shelves of leather backed books edged in gold. I said honestly, "No, sister." Then she clarified herself, "Do you have books at home?" "Oh yes, we have books." I loved books but I didn't want to be seen as a bookworm, or worse an egghead.

It was one thing to have Sister Damian tell me that I looked like a teacher in third grade, but quite another to think I might look like one in eighth grade. I needed a makeover. So I decided before I went to the new school that I should change my name to *Suzanne* because *Suzanne* was French and seemed sophisticated to me. I wanted so desperately to be accepted into the "in" crowd. I practiced writing *Suzanne*. Yes, the "z" made all the difference. It would bring pizazz into my dull persona. However, as my wise Grandmother B used to say, "You can't make a silk purse out of a sow's ear." She was so right.

Emily Dowd, Barbara Johnson, Susan, Kathy Fisk
Birthday luncheon October 18, 1954
Red Bank, NJ

In eighth grade I went to St. James Grammar School. The school was overcrowded so a house had been converted into classrooms for the eighth grade: Eight A was upstairs and Eight B was downstairs. This was different from the regular school with long corridors and square classrooms and that made it fun. One day in early September, I was standing under a tree by myself when a young girl came up to me and said, "Hi, I'm Joan." That was the simple beginning of a friendship that has lasted over fifty years. My new friend's mom made the obligatory visit to my mom before I was allowed to stay overnight. From then on Joan and I were inseparable. I was invited to join the Catholic Daughters of America her mother had organized. It was sort of like Girl Scouts. We were expected to be good Catholics girls and do good deeds. At last I was part of a group.

**Graduation from St. James Grammar School
Red Bank, NJ 1955**

During our first summer as friends, Joan and I helped Sister
Jacobe run a morning program at Nativity Parish in Fair Haven.
This was also our first experience working with children. Our long
careers in education had begun. In the afternoons, Joan's mom
would drive us to the beach. We'd help lug and set up chairs, umbrel-
las and paraphernalia for six people and one baby. Then we'd spend
hours swimming and riding the waves, stopping only to ravenously

eat delicious sandwiches and snacks. When we weren't in the water, we were talking. Talking as only teenage girls can talk. We talked about boys. We talked about our friends, our teachers, boys, our parents, our siblings, our worries and we talked about what we'd do after high school. And we talked about boys. At four o'clock we'd help pack up the car, and I'd be dropped off at my house. Because my mother didn't drive, I was always grateful that Mrs. Held was willing to go out of her way for me.

———◦◦◦———

I realized very quickly that I could not change my personality by changing my name. Try as I might. I would remain "Susan" or even plain "Sue." I'd hang out with people I felt comfortable with even if they weren't as exciting or flashy or as much fun as the "in" crowd seemed to be. Most of the graduates of St. James moved right on to Red Bank Catholic High School, also taught by the Sisters of Mercy. Even so, I still suffered a million agonies standing outside the new high school waiting for the doors to open for the first day back. And I felt this way every single September, no matter how many friends or acquaintances I made. Reentry was always painful.

I started going to Mass every day; something that my friend Joan did as well. Our dads dropped us off on their way to work at Fort Monmouth. I felt at home in the quiet, darkened church before the service. The votive candles flickered peacefully. The large red candle hung in front of the tabernacle because Jesus was present. That's what Sister said. I was in the presence of God and he loved me. I was never really alone, and it didn't matter if I had a boyfriend or if I wasn't as popular as I wanted to be. But in truth, people did like me. My sometimes reserved, pious looking exterior hid a smart aleck teenager who was always ready with under the breath quips and *sotto voce* wisecracks during class. One teacher got tired of my shenanigans and called on me to stand in front of the class and read an embarrassing stanza of poetry that had the dreaded word "breast" in it. As my face reddened appropriately in front of a co-ed class, she knew I got the intended message: "Knock it off."

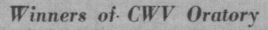
Winners of CWV Oratory

Susan Bassler of Red Bank and Hans Ziegler of Elberon, Red Bank Catholic high school students, won the fifth annual oratorical contest sponsored by the county Catholic War Veterans last week in St. Rose high school, Belmar. They are shown receiving prizes from Thomas F. Salmon, county CWV commander, left, and Frank L. Innacelli, county CWV vice commander and contest chairman, extreme right. 'How Can I as a Youth Lead the Way?' was the subject of the five-minute orations. Judges were Rev. William J. Bausch, New Monmouth; Col. Harrison C. Travis, USA Ret., Fair Haven; Donald J. Cunningham, Jr., Avon borough attorney; William P. Diviney, personnel management division at Ft. Monmouth, and William J. Brennan, chief of civilian training at Ft. Monmouth.

Susan Bassler & Hans Ziegler *Red Bank Register* March 26,1959

My brother was a top-notch debater; he and his team won many debates in local and national contests. So with his urging, I joined the school's National Catholic Forensic League. Besides debates, it sponsored local, state and national contests in oratory, poetry and drama. I memorized and delivered famous speeches and I also wrote my own. I actually went to Washington, D.C. with a busload of students representing New Jersey's best Catholic orators. But because one of the best Catholic orators was a black girl, we were seated in the farthest, darkest corner of a restaurant. I felt ashamed. Just as I had when we drove to Baltimore to visit my brother and stopped at a roadside store to get a bite to eat. The sign on the counter told Negros to take their food outside and eat at the picnic tables.

Catholic High Recaptures Temple Trophy

Front: Alfred Westerfield, Rita Belcher, Pamela Marzulla, Joan Held,
Susan Bassler, Margaret Fisk, Margaret Howlett
Back: Daniel Malcolm, Michael Costura, Paul Cullen, John Breickner,
Michael Dowell

All this public speaking should have made me less shy, yet before many a contest I'd ask myself why in the world was I putting myself through this agony? Even though I was very busy with many Forensic contests like the Temple University tournament, I also joined the Sodality, a group for girls that fosters in its members a devotion and reverence towards the Blessed Virgin Mary. Actually, I joined two Sodalities: one at St. James Parish and one at the high school. I was active in both and held various offices. The priest in charge of the high school sodality sent all of the officers to a conference in Worcester in the summer before our senior year. We had a great time. Always the chronicler, I kept notes on Hotel Bancroft stationary from July 13-18 and still have them. Joan and I invited a Mary Walton to room with us because she had come alone. On Thursday evening instead of going to Talent Night I went with Mary to visit Sr. Mary Joan at the convent of Notre Dame. Mary was also thinking about becoming a nun, and we corresponded during senior year. The next summer Mary met a boy and changed her mind about becoming a sister. I have often wondered if that had happened to me, would I be writing this memoir.

Mary Walton, Gladys O'Keefe, Gail McGrail & Cora, two girls from Maine, Pat Farrer, Pat Zambrano, Joan Held
Holy Cross College Worcester, Massachusetts 1958

Sophomore year I auditioned for the school play, *Brigadoon* and in senior year I was in *The Boy Friend*. I also had great fun in *Side by Side*, the Senior variety show, organized by Sr. Vincent as a class fundraiser. And I studied. Only once did I achieve the Honor Roll of Distinction, which meant that you had received an "A" in all subjects.

My father looked at my report card and said: "OK, you showed them you could do it." Clearly, he did not expect me to do that every marking period. The pressure was off. But I always made Honor Roll.

Except once. We had a gym teacher, Mrs. Repka, whom I sarcastically called "Mrs. Reptile." She also was in charge of a health class. I can't bring myself, even now, to say she taught it. The accepted practice was to lay your health book on your lap during a test. I found this distasteful as well as dishonest, and I wouldn't do it. However, I also didn't study for the test, which I failed. For me it became a test of wills or maybe I liked the attention of being a whistle blower on the health teacher's suspect pedagogy. Anyway, my parents were called to school. I felt very righteous. But in the end, I had to retake the test. The poor grade in Health lowered my grade point average and the incident kept me off the National Honor Society- for life! It also shows how insufferable I could be.

Susan in costume for *The Boy Friend*

My friend, Joan, had the use of a car during high school so we'd go to the movies or to Saturday football games and then head to the Pizza Parlor afterwards. I even bought a pack of cigarettes from a machine and lit up. But as luck would have it, I dropped an ash on the front of my synthetic Japanese blouse, which left a telltale hole and ended my interest in smoking. My efforts at sophistication always fizzled. I don't remember any sermons against smoking. My dad smoked a pipe and my mother had an elegant black cigarette holder, which I remember her using when she tried to teach my brother and me how to play bridge. I would never dream of using that.

We tried bowling and one Saturday morning a few of us even went horseback riding. And of course there were school dances. When I was a sophomore, my brother went to St. Charles College in Catonsville, Maryland to become a parish priest. I missed him terribly, but we wrote frequently, sometimes in schoolbook French, and visited as often as we could. When I was a senior, he left the seminary and even taught briefly at Red Bank Catholic High School before going to Fordham.

—◦◦◦—

Socializing started in 8th grade. Many students, including my best friend, took couples' dance lessons at a woman's home. They also participated in dinners where the boys learned to open a door for a lady and to pull out a woman's chair at the table. The girls learned to smile and say "thank you." It probably didn't cost a lot, but my parents had just bought a house and there was no discretionary money. So I had to learn to smile and say "thank you" on my own. But the house parties started then as well, and being new, I was not invited to those either.

In high school the good sisters felt it was part of their mission to prepare us for a refined social life. Finishing schools were a thing of the past. So Sr. Eleanor, the Principal, instituted Freshmen Teas. These were afternoon affairs. Since we wore ugly green gabardine uniforms most of the time, it was a welcome chance to wear our prettiest dresses that needed flouncy petticoats. We had to wear white cotton gloves. The boys always wore jackets, shirts and ties to class anyway but they had to shine their shoes and look spiffy. The girls had dance cards. I walked around with great pleading in my eyes for a boy, any boy, to sign up for a dance. If you didn't have any blanks, lucky you, which usually meant your real boyfriend, filled up your card. But if you were me, then those blanks would look like railroad lines stretching into eternity. Except I knew no train was going to pull into my station. In that case, it was time to go to the bathroom to powder my nose or go to the punch bowl with the other wallflowers. The poor intimidated boys had to make sure they found a girl with an empty blank and would walk around solemnly looking for a match-up. If they weren't born with natural rhythm (highly unlikely in a predominantly Irish school with a few Italians thrown in); if they didn't have a sister who would practice with them as my brother did with me; or if they were absent when the gym teacher went quickly over the dance steps — then they were doomed.

Once, a decent enough fellow approached me for dance number three. Yes, his name was there. I checked my dance card again and yes, indeed, this was my partner. We stepped away from the wall and into the arena - Christians to the lions. He took my gloved hand in his, clutching the dance card, and proceeded to move. He pumped away with his right arm that in turn made his right foot move forward. My left arm of course pumped right along with his. It was not an intricate dance step, and he stuck with it for the entire song. Up and down. Up and down. We proceeded around the perimeter of the gym like a hand truck on my Grandfather's B & O Railroad reminiscent of a scene from *Oh Brother Where Art Thou*. When the music mercifully stopped, my number three-dance card signatory quickly returned me to my starting point.

Snowball 1958

There were ordinary dances as well, given by this school club or that to raise money. The lights were considerably dimmer. One time, a young man I didn't recognize approached and I followed him out onto the floor for a slow dance. He held me tight, too tight for my comfort. When I expressed no interest in going to a rock concert with him, he returned me to my spot by the wall. I liked boys but the ones I was attracted to didn't return the favor. I tried flirting with one handsome young man I sat next to in history class. When I inquired where he was the following year I was told he had entered the seminary.

I did have a group of friends. We weren't in any of the favored cliques portrayed so well in the *Breakfast Club*. We just gravitated toward each other into the black hole of the dateless semi-nerds. Nice enough folks. Alcohol was never involved. We'd get together for parties at each other's homes - places that had finished recreation rooms-a basement with paneling and a rug- were popular in the 50's. Usually parents didn't go down to the "rec" room; so for many, it was a potential "near occasion of sin." which Sister defined: "as any person, place or thing that may easily lead one into sin." Which in nun-speak meant boys, boys and boys. We'd play 45's that were banned by the Legion of Decency like Jerry Lewis' *Whole Lotta Shakin' Goin On* or Margie Rayburn's *I'm Available*. I remember having one party at my home where we very definitely didn't play banned records. My parents rolled up my grandmother's braided rugs so we could dance. I couldn't let my hair down with my parents listening upstairs. I hope somebody had fun. I didn't.

I didn't have a steady boyfriend either. This caused endless problems that culminated in literally my last dance. The Prom. This phenomenon may have started as the poor people's debutante ball. Maybe, it was designed to be a young woman's last hurrah before proposals and marriage. Proms are very expensive on every conceivable level - from the cost of the dress and shoes, to the cost of flowers and limo. But these costs are nothing compared to the psychological cost to the boy of asking and risking a refusal or the cost to the girl of not being asked by the right boy or not being asked at all. I can still see myself sitting by the phone waiting for a call.

It came eventually and I said, "Yes" to Jim but my heart was not in it. I have always suspected the nuns put him up to it.

The Prom June 1959

We were forbidden to wear strapless gowns. So my mother sewed on pink spaghetti straps to the most gorgeous dress I have ever owned. Most of the students drove down to the convent before the prom so the Sisters could make sure we were dressed properly. Now I realize they probably just enjoyed seeing us dressed up and seeing with whom we were matched-up. I double dated with Jim and his friend, Donald who had a car, and off we went to the Hotel Berkely in Asbury Park. Later they dropped us off in Red Bank where there wasn't anything open so we walked forlornly back to my house. Perhaps Jim got a kiss good night, but I don't remember. I do remember lamenting the whole sorry thing with my mother. The next day I put on my white Peter Pan blouse and green gabardine jumper and went to school as usual. More like Sleeping Beauty than Cinderella, I was still waiting for a Prince's kiss that would arouse me from my slumber of innocence.

—⟨ɷɷɷ⟩—

Much has been said and written about the role of the good sisters in the formation of Catholics. Until the recent pedophilia debacle, less has been said of the role of the priest. It is difficult to think of the exalted place the parish priest played in the life of Catholics without it now being tainted with "the scandal." In fact, it has been pointed out to me that perhaps the sisters themselves contributed to "the scandal" because they fostered a godlike attitude toward "Father." I find that line of reasoning incredible. Although it is true that whenever a priest entered the classroom, sister would tell us to stand for Father and say "Thank you, Father" and "Good afternoon, Father." He was also dressed in a long, black flowing garment – a cassock, but we learned early on that he had more power. Students could almost feel and taste sister's deference and respect for the collar. God and the Church spoke through the priest. And although it was hard to tell, even second graders knew that he was a man and she was a woman.

For Catholics of a certain age, the *Baltimore Catechism* held all the answers. We memorized it. By second grade, we knew that only a priest administered the sacraments, baptized babies and heard confessions, gave out Holy Communion, married and buried people and was a priest forever. The idea of Confession was frightening. But I couldn't make my First Communion without making my First Confession. Of course, the sisters prepared us for this momentous day, but the idea still scared me. I had a lot to remember. And my sins were the least of it. First the priest would slide open the window, and then I would say: "Bless me Father for I have sinned. This is my first confession. I sassed my mother two times. I got mad at my brother five times, and I forgot to pick up my room once." Father would say something like: "All right my child. For your penance say one Our Father and One Hail Mary. Now say the Act of Contrition." "O my God I am heartily sorry for having offended thee..." The little window would slide shut and it was over. I would scurry red-faced back to the pew and say my penance and by the end of it my heart was beating normally. After the trauma of Saturday's confession, receiving communion on Sunday was joyous, once I got past the people staring at me. I walked up to the altar rail, knelt down, tilted my head back, closed my eyes, stuck out my tongue and Father gave me Jesus.

Once in third grade I confessed that I had missed Mass on Sunday. This I knew was a mortal sin. Of course I hadn't missed Mass, and I don't know why I said it, except that I was always nervous going to confession, and I guess I momentarily forgot my list. Anyway, the priest got very upset and threatened to expel me from Catholic school. I don't remember my penance. I was eight.

Sister told us about the Last Judgment. We would be judged immediately after we died, but at the end of the world there would be one big reckoning. Everybody would be there and all your sins would be paraded in front of everyone. This thought terrified me more than death itself. Everybody would know everything! This thought acted as a great inhibitor. The Last Judgment kept me from doing forbidden things or even thinking any forbidden thoughts right through the turbulent, pubescent teens. However, something did happen when we moved to the duplex in Long Branch that caused me great emotional pain for a couple of years. A slightly older girl who lived next door invited me over. We were in her bedroom talking when she told me she had witnessed renters making out and having sex. She then proceeded to show me by climbing on top of me and moving up and down as she had seen the man do. We were fully clothed, and I in no way wanted to do something bad, yet I felt I had. I never went to her house again. I never told anyone. I certainly did not want to tell a priest in confession. So I didn't. But therein lay the torture. I compounded the sin every time I went to communion and every time I went to confession and hid the secret. The mortal sins were piling up. I was able to suppress the whole memory for a while, and I made my confirmation, but eventually I did find the courage to confess something that fell under the sixth or ninth commandment. My relief was enormous. I would make sure that in the future I would do nothing that I couldn't tell Father in the confessional.

—cⁿ/ⁿ/ⁿ⸗—

There are vocations and avocations. An avocation is a hobby, something you might do for fun like cooking or painting. A vocation is serious. It is something you feel passionately about and will dedicate your whole being to pursue it. In our society, it might be teaching or it might be any of the helping professions like nursing or social work. In the Catholic Church the word vocation has a very specific meaning. It is a call from God to serve him as a sister, a brother or a priest. It is the duty of religious to foster or encourage vocations. So as I have mentioned, in sixth grade I went with other girls to visit a motherhouse.

The idea that I might have a vocation was not foreign to me. In fact in grammar school, I had sent away for information and brochures about various communities, probably as a school assignment during Vocation Month. I remember reading about the Sisters of the Blessed Sacrament who had schools for Negro and Native American children in the south and west. I had a brochure from the Maryknoll Sisters, an American group that did foreign missionary work. I found both attractive. I remember riding my bike around the neighborhood thinking I needed to have a healthy body if I were going to do missionary work in a far-a-way land. Occasionally, sisters and brothers from various orders would preach from the pulpit about the work that they did. I always thought they were looking directly at me as they spoke.

Sometimes, I felt I was living a double life; certainly not as duplicitous as Herb Philbrick in the popular TV show *I Led Three Lives*, but nearly as destructive. I was participating fully in the life of a high school student and having fun, but at other times I was struggling with overwhelming life issues. In junior year on a Saturday morning, I went with hundreds of other young people to take the SAT's. I hadn't bothered to take the Saturday morning prep classes that the sisters provided. Nor had anyone suggested I should. I hadn't gone to the Guidance Counselor to talk about colleges. Nor had the counselor called me in to find out what I was going to do with myself after high school. I had done well in top academic classes; yet I did not send out applications to colleges; nor did I try for scholarships as my brother had done; nor did my parents encourage it. I had been gradually burning my bridges. My parents never brought up the topic of college. They never discussed finances. My brother was going to be a senior in Fordham so he needed support. My parents never suggested I work for a year. My mother and I fought about everything, even who was playing the correct time in a piano duet. But we did not fight about whether I was going to college or not. On the other hand, we did have exhausting, sustained fights about my leaving home and going into the Ursulines. At one point my father said; "If you don't leave now you never will." It wasn't like I didn't see examples of female independence. Gladys, another close friend, who had already started a joint savings account with her boyfriend, worked and went to a state teachers college in New Jersey.

Independence hadn't been fostered in my life. During my freshman summer I could have had a steady job babysitting at a beach club where my brother parked cars, but my parents felt I was too young. I did have a few babysitting jobs during high school, but I didn't exude confidence even there. I remember one young child looked up at me and said: "You don't do this very much do you?" For at least half of my adult life, anger and resentment about my parents' attitude toward my education festered, barely disguised. When I finally brought up the subject many years later, my mother said: "Well, we couldn't afford to send you to Georgian Court." This was the college run by the Sisters of Mercy. And to support his position, my father looked to a German engineer he worked with, who also wasn't sending his daughter to college because, he argued, there was no need to invest in a girl who will be married in a few years. But since my own mother had been given the opportunity to attend Pittsburgh Music Institute in the 1930's, this was hardly a valid argument in the late 1950's. However, I have a harder time coming to grips with my own position. My extreme passivity is puzzlement to me, even now.

Prefect of St. James Sodality May crowning 1959

Although I felt friendly toward a couple of my high school teachers, I never thought seriously about becoming a Sister of Mercy. I
didn't see them as holy enough. Remember underneath it all, I still
had aspirations for sainthood. I gradually began to think that I too
had a vocation - that God was calling me to be a sister. If I did
indeed have a vocation, then there was no question that I would
obey God's will and become a nun. But how would I know? And
what kind of nun would I become? These things were talked about
in Religion class and the Sodalities I participated in particularly
during Vocation Month. If you really thought you had a vocation,
then you should find a priest who you could talk to outside of confession. Even now if you search for vocations.com on the web, you

will find information that hasn't changed in fifty years. A priest, you're told, will give you spiritual direction and help you discern if your vocation is legitimate.

I was shy. I really didn't want to do this, but if it was what God wanted for me, then I'd have to do it. My best friend had the same dilemma. Our parish was large. It was headed by a Monsignor and assisted by three parish priests who also taught senior religion at our high school. My friend chose the priest who ran the high school Sodality. As Robert Frost has said so well: "Two roads diverged in a yellow wood..." I chose a different priest and that made all the difference in the rest of my life. I chose a priest who I thought was serious and holy and not particularly popular-Father August Neumann. Once a week I'd steal over to the rectory for my spiritual direction. I didn't want to be seen walking up the steep granite stairs to the rectory door, so instead of walking down Broad Street, I'd go behind the church, through the parking lot, and dart up the rectory driveway. I'd ring the doorbell, and be let in by the housekeeper. I felt uneasy. Rectories still make me feel edgy. No wonder my mother didn't want to be married in a rectory. There is a quiet, dead, flatness to them that is disconcerting. They do not have the normal smells and sounds of a home. I'd be ushered into a small parlor where I'd sit and wait for Father. Pleasantries would be exchanged. He would ask questions about my week. As the year wore on he'd ask about more personal things.

"Which parent are you closer to?" he's ask.

"My, father," I'd answer.

"Which parent would you go to if you had a question or a problem?"

"Well, I'd go to my father for most things. But if it was about religion, I guess I'd ask my mother." His response was a nod.

Once he commented on how red my lipstick was. Did he think I had a boyfriend? In hindsight, I cynically think perhaps he was concerned that the fish would shake the hook before he landed the catch.

I still wasn't sure what kind of a sister I wanted to be. Although I was sure I didn't want to be a nurse, like Sr. Athanasius, our biology teacher. I liked her because she once apologized to our class for being sarcastic. It was the first time I had heard anyone in authority do that and I respected her immensely. I liked her enough to spend afternoons helping her move unsold Valentine candy into Mother's Day boxes. She trusted me with this secret, and I didn't even tell my mother the real reason I was coming home late from school.

Religious communities are generally founded to solve a particular problem and fill a need. Members wear distinctive habits usually what had been worn when the community was founded in the 1700s or 1800s and were never changed. That applies to women. Brothers and priests no matter what community they belong to wear a cassock usually black sometimes brown. Communities also have different Holy Rules and Constitutions that guide their daily lives. Most Catholics have vague ideas about all of this and know only the groups with which they are familiar. Non-Catholics have to rely on TV or the movies: Sally Field in *The Flying Nun* or the German sisters in *Lilies of the Field*, or Julie Andrews in *The Sound of Music*, or *Nunsense*, or *Sister Act*. So while my contemporaries were visiting campuses, I went with Father on his day off to check out different convents whose parlors felt as flat and lifeless as rectories. Choosing a convent where I would spend the rest of my life was not going to be easy.

My parents knew, of course, that I was going on Saturday jaunts with Father. Once I remember sitting in an enormous parlor with high ceilings and tall windows overlooking the Hudson River. It may have been the Franciscan motherhouse at Hastings on Hudson, but I could not see myself there. Another time, Father pulled up outside the walls of Sing Sing. I suppose he wanted to show me a famous landmark of Ossining. I stared at the forbidding walls in silence - dumbfounded. A Freudian could probably connect the dots. I guess we had been up to see the Maryknoll motherhouse. Sometimes we would stop by and pick up his elderly mother for lunch. Finally, he took me out to Blue Point, Long Island. He had been taught in grammar school by the Ursuline Sisters of Tildonk. He must have been a difficult student because he told me they once locked him in the cloakroom closet for misbehaving, but he climbed out the window and took off. He had great respect for these women. Perhaps he took me there as a recruit because he felt he had an unpaid debt to them. Perhaps he'd made a promise that if he ever came across a fitting candidate he would steer her to their community as reparations for all the grief he had given them. I knew about the Ursulines who ran the College of New Rochelle, but I would never have heard about this particular group of Ursulines from Belgium unless Father had introduced them to me. That is how I found myself sitting in another large parlor, but this time I felt different. The sisters were pleased to see Father and chatted amiably. We had lunch in a small room near the parlor. We visited the small Chapel and walked in the garden. I met the Novice Mistress, a young woman with a beautiful smile. I could see myself in this convent.

When my mother found out that I was probably going to enter the Ursuline Convent in Blue Point, she was very upset. And she sprang into action. Reminiscent of her mother's march to Sister Bertha years earlier, my mother boldly went down to the rectory and spoke directly to Father Neumann. There was no love lost between them, yet neither one of them divulged this encounter to me at the time. It probably wouldn't have made a difference. I most certainly would have been angry with my mother for interfering. Everyone was trying to operate within the parameters of "God's Will." But if you knew my mother, you might agree that what she did was selfless and bordered on the heroic.

I made a few more visits to Blue Point during school vacations. On Fridays January 2nd and April 3rd I took the train to Penn Station and then the Long Island Railroad to Blue Point. On April 17th my friend, Joan, came with me for an overnight. Finally, my parents and I made the trip together. My parents were not happy. My mother was very, very unhappy. The Ursulines were semi-cloistered religious, and unlike the Sisters of Mercy the Ursulines did not permit visits home – ever. They did allow parents to visit a few times a year, but Blue Point was at least a three-hour one way trip from Red Bank, New Jersey with most of it on the dreaded Long Island Expressway. My friend, Joan, had decided to join the Sisters of Mercy. Their motherhouse was only an hour away in Plainfield, New Jersey. I was going to choose the Ursulines just because they were the greater challenge. If I were going to sacrifice my life to God, then I would make the grand gesture. I could be insufferable. I also had secret, inner bargains to make with God. I wanted my dad to really convert and really become a practicing Catholic and to go to confession and receive Holy Communion like a real Catholic. I thought God would reward my sacrifice and make this happen.

I can see myself walking up the large granite stairs to the Post Office to mail my letter to Reverend Mother Ursula, the Superior of the Ursulines of Tildonk in Blue Point, Long Island, New York. I had made the decision, and I had written it down. The die was cast. I knew where I was going in September. I knew I was leaving home never to return. I knew I was going to become a sister no matter what it took. So once I had licked the stamp, I had literally sealed my fate. I had given my word for better or worse, even though during the summer I had second thoughts. Nothing could be done. I had sent the letter. I had a way of seeing everything in black and white. Years earlier, my father had shown me the binary system that would run computers. Everything was a One or a Zero. That's how I thought. No room for compromise. No room for indecision. No going back. In July and August I began giving away things to my friends. I would soon be dead to the world.

We lived by the ocean, and I found comfort in the rhythm and strength of the waves. I wrote a poem.

In pensive silence I watched the sea below
Dark, vast, and limitless
Unending waves pounded, pounded, pounded
I yearned to leap
But
Sudden death restrained me
So terrified at being lost in immensity unbounded
I clutched the soft steel bar of self
And wondered
At the endless beating, beating, beating of the Heart of God
Such constant ageless love o'erwhelmed me
The moon so warm, so reassuring shone above
Dissolved my fears
And I plunged into Love.

But before I would take myself out of the world, my parents wanted me to have memories. I didn't feel at the time that they were trying to change my mind by showing me what the world had to offer, but perhaps they were. They took me to a very posh restaurant with a view of the Hudson River. In the ladies' room, a woman sat on a stool waiting to hand out linen towels to dry one's hands. I felt very uncomfortable with that, and I felt bad for the woman who had to sit in a bathroom all day. They took me to see *The Music Man* - my first Broadway show, and I loved it. After graduation we made one last trip to Butler, Pennsylvania to visit my Grandparents. I have a picture of me and my mother and dad standing in our dining room and toasting each other with a glass of sparkling burgundy. It was memorable because when my dad uncorked the wine, it popped with a vengeance and hit the ceiling. Little spots of red were splattered everywhere. My mother was not happy about that. In fact I am the only one smiling in this picture of the last supper.

Mom, Dad, Susan   September 1959

I received a letter from the Ursuline Motherhouse with a list of things I would need to bring with me. I was going to become a bride of Christ, and I needed to come prepared. In my family such wedding preparations had been called a Hope Chest and took a few years to complete. My grandmother had made sure that my mother entered marriage with all the essentials of setting up house, and they worked on it together. Tablecloths and napkins, sheets and pillowcases were decorated with hand embroidery. Handkerchiefs were edged in homemade tatting. My grandmother even made sure my mother's teeth were seen to so the newly married couple wouldn't have that expense. The ancient bride price had morphed into the dowry that had become the Hope Chest, which in my case had turned into the list for the Trunk. My friend and I actually made our long white flannel nightgowns on a sewing machine my mother had given me for Christmas. After that the Singer was put into a closet.

I had been assigned a number when my letter arrived from Blue Point. That number was 55. I ordered labels and sewed them onto everything that would be laundered. But there were other things a nun needed in her wardrobe that could only be found in a special shop in New York City. So on a lovely morning in June, my mother and I took the bus to the Big Apple. We met with my future Novice Mistress at the appointed store and purchased items that we had never seen before: underwear that looked like bloomers, long cotton slips, cotton camisoles instead of bras, cotton handkerchiefs. But the strangest item on the list was a silver-folding pen knife. I could see that my mother was annoyed at the price, but it was on the list so she reluctantly bought it. After all, I wasn't going to disobey Mother Superior before I had even entered the convent. Perhaps in Belgium a nun needed it to pare fruit or sharpen pencils. As a kid I was pretty good at playing mumbly peg, but as a nun I never ever used it, and wish I knew what happened to it.

My mother and I parted with the Novice Mistress and took the subway uptown to Radio City Music Hall. My mother was trying to put a positive spin on what for her was a dreary day and also provide me with another lasting memory, which she accomplished. I had been to Radio City Music Hall before, but I still looked in awe at the vast Art

Deco lobby and I loved watching the Rockettes. They are just amazing. Finally, the big curtain parted and the movie began – *The Nun's Story*. What a coincidence. What irony. The movie starring Audrey Hepburn was riveting. My mother and I lost in our own thoughts said little on our bus ride back to Red Bank.

Sister Vincent, my history teacher who was the moderator of the National Catholic Forensic League, knew that I had seen *The Nun's Story*. She wanted me to know that it accurately portrayed life in the convent and said to me: "You know, Susan, that's the way it is." I didn't really believe her. She might have tried to change my mind about going into the Ursulines; but to her credit, she didn't. The Sisters of Mercy really didn't need me. Their vocations were flourishing. It seemed whole basketball teams were entering their community. Maybe Father Neumann had said; "Hands off. This one is mine."

I bought a foot locker to pack all the sheets and blankets, nightgowns, black stockings, black nun shoes, a black shawl and other things that that been on my list. Everything was either black or white. After graduation the summer seemed to fly by. I do remember experiencing one panic moment over my decision. I said something to my brother about my doubts, but it was just a passing wave not big enough to knock me down. September finally arrived.

———◦∅∅◦———

On September 8, 1959, the Feast of the Nativity of the Blessed Virgin, my family and I got into the car, a jazzy two tone, blue and white Buick. My Grandfather Kerr had owned a Buick when dad was courting my mom and owning one had been on his to-do list for over twenty years. However, I was self-conscious about stepping out of such a fancy car when dad dropped me off for Mass before school. As someone soon to embrace a life of poverty, I didn't think it suited me. Nonetheless, that is the car that took us up the Garden State to the Long Island Expressway and out to Blue Point. I would be living there for the next six years.

After 103 miles we pulled into the gravel driveway and got out and joined the other parents and girls gathering in the garden. We walked the pine tree lined paths past the large grotto, a replica of the one in Lourdes where St. Bernadette saw the Blessed Mother, and a small raised cemetery. After everyone had arrived, the Novice Mistress took all the newcomers inside. I was taken to a room and given the clothes that a postulant would wear. We went back to the garden and pictures were taken and then my family left. I had done it. I had entered the convent.

Before   **Entrance Day September 8, 1959**   **After**

The word "postulant" comes from the Latin *postulans, postulanti* and the present participle of *postulare*, to demand. Ironically, the first thing a postulant learns is NOT to demand anything. In high school students were tested and placed into homogeneous classes. The convent's approach is different. It is called rank. We had all been assigned numbers with the date of our acceptance. Mine, you will recall, was 55. Ninita, a young woman from Connecticut who arrived a week late due to injuries sustained in a car accident lost her place and was forever last- right behind me. We became good friends. Anytime there was a line-up, all eight postulants took their places according to rank, as did all the novices and all the professed sisters. We sat in the Chapel in that order. We walked to the refectory in that order. We sat at the dining table in that order. We even sat at recreation in that order. My father, the former Lutheran, would refer humorously to where I lived as "the big house" his euphemism for prison.

—*⟋⟋⟋*—

I can only imagine the ride home for my parents and brother. Did my mother clutch the bag of clothes knowing her only daughter would never put them on again? Years later she told me that when she looked at my eyelash curler in the medicine cabinet she would burst into tears. Did they blame themselves? Did they blame each other? Did they blame Catholic education? I don't think there would have been much conversation but my mother probably cried. My brother told me everyone was depressed.

I didn't have time for tears. The Novice Mistress and the Assistant Novice Mistress kept us very busy, and at first it was all exciting. I had battled my parents to enter, and that had taken a lot of energy. I had battled my own doubts and fears, and that had taken a lot of courage. I did not know the battles with perseverance that lay ahead. I was on my way. I had done it, and there was much to learn. I called the Novice Mistress "Mother," even though she was only eleven years older than I was. It was her duty to teach me how to become an Ursuline. She taught me the proper way to walk, to hold my hands, to kneel when the Mother Superior stopped me in the corridor, to be silent, to clean-convent style, to speak in a soft voice. There were rules and there were schedules. There was little time to be homesick.

The Ursuline's had purchased the John Senger estate in 1935 to be the community's motherhouse and novitiate. Fronting Middle Road it was only blocks from the Great South Bay. When Mother Ursula arrived in 1948 she added a two-story wing at the back that housed the large refectory on the first floor and the novitiate overhead on the second floor. On the first floor toward the front were the parlors, and a guest dining room and bathroom. The chapel was at that end of the building as was the small library. Toward the back, was the large refectory or dining room and a spacious commercial kitchen. Roughly forty women were at the motherhouse at any one time. The professed sisters had private bedrooms on the second floor. Each room was furnished with a single bed, chair, night table and lamp. The individual rooms for the postulants were in one wing of the building. In the dormitory, which had also been renovated by Mother Ursula, the first and second year novices slept in individual curtained cubicles. The novitiate was a large sunny room on the second floor with a sun porch that had banks of windows looking out to the water. The sewing room and the offices for the Reverend Mother and her assistant were outside of the novitiate. Downstairs the basement was a warren of different compartments: a laundry room, a bread room, and a walk- in cooler. Another section had small partitioned spaces with pianos in them - practice rooms. Rumor had it that a secret passage existed allowing a priest to go from the Chapel to the outside. But I never saw it. A postulant or a sister traveled to various parts of the house when she was told to. There was no wandering around out of idle curiosity.

I am a morning person, so the early rising at 6:30 didn't bother me, but that was a whole hour after the professed sisters got up. Postulants were given certain concessions to allow them to ease into the monastic life. There were prayers to say when putting on each article of clothing. Mass was at 7:00 followed by the rosary in the garden. If the weather didn't permit that, then I could walk the corridors or remain in the Chapel. That gave fifteen precious minutes to the novices in charge of getting breakfast ready. Breakfast was taken in silence followed by prayers in the chapel. Postulants and novices did the dishes. And everyone did chores. Fifteen minutes of spiritual reading was followed by an hour of study for a college math lesson lasting another hour, and then dinner. Dinner was at noon, a European tradition. On Sundays and Holy Days the Mother Vicar rang a bell; we could talk until she rang it again, and then we were silent. A novice read from the lectern during silence. After the meal the servers cleared the table and we processed in rank to the chapel. Then we had recreation for an hour, outdoors if it was nice. Sometimes we played baseball. Talking! There would be afternoon tea in silence and then study or afternoon chores, which might be peeling potatoes, putting out the wash, dusting or sweeping the long corridors with a green compound, or brushing down the stairs. At 4 PM we would go to the Chapel for Vespers, followed by quiet

time, then supper at 5:00, Chapel again, and dishes. We had recreation for an hour up in the novitiate room, where we could talk
while we sorted stamps or learned how to darn our black stockings.
My grandmother used to say: "Idle hands are the devils' workshop."
There are no idle hands in a convent. At 8:00 we would go to the
chapel for evening prayers and Compline and then up to our rooms,
shower and bed. I took off my postulant outfit as carefully as I had
put it on and hung my veil on the corner of a straight back chair. I
turned over the rug by my bed and turned down the white cotton
counterpane. Because of the Great Silence there was no chatting.
Speaking to anyone in the corridor or going to another's room was
strictly forbidden. An older sister would walk by our open doors
and say to each postulant in French, "Luis Sois Jesu Christ." (Praise
be Jesus Christ) I would respond "A Jamais." (Forever and ever)
One postulant didn't quite get the French; so it came out "As you
may." There was no late night reading or studying but everybody
was pretty exhausted anyway. And a new day would begin soon
enough.

The convent had an arrangement with St John's University.
We were enrolled in the evening school at a special rate for religious. This allowed us to begin accruing credits while still at the
motherhouse, which was forward thinking by this community.
Many teaching orders sent very young women into the classroom without any training, and they were expected to attend
college part time. I was lucky. Once a week, a priest from St.
John's University would come to teach a theology course. Some
of our own sisters were qualified to teach 101 courses. On Sat-
urdays we had Church History and Bible History lessons. We
completed six college credits as postulants. Sr. Joseph was our
Director of Studies.

Saturday was also laundry day. We helped the novices. The
wash would be taken out of industrial washers and put in a large
spinner and then carried outside and hung up. As the weather
got colder this became more difficult. Later we'd go out and bring
in the wash to the folding room. This was a large room in the
basement with several long tables, ironing boards and a mangle
for sheets. Everything got folded and placed into piles according

to the number sewn onto the clothing. The novices also ironed the bandeaux heavily starched rectangular linens with two ties to be folded to fit each sister's head. The veil was attached to this. Everyone wore fresh clothes on Sunday.

Sunday started a little later in the morning. Again the novices and professed were in the Chapel meditating before the postulants arrived. Matins would be chanted and Mass would follow, after that the rosary would be said in the garden. When the bell rang all would process to the refectory and have breakfast. We ate very well. Breakfast varied. On ordinary mornings it might be toast, cereal and milk with a small glass of orange juice. On Sundays or Holy Days it would consist of coffee or tea, (the Irish sisters always had tea) baked eggs and bacon and rolls and butter. A Belgium custom was to serve good rolls and butter with chocolate. We'd have a Nestlé bar for the same effect. Sometimes, if it were a feast day, the bell would ring and we could talk. After dishes and Chapel the postulants and novices went up to the novitiate to study the Catechism for half an hour. The biography of the founder, Rev. John Lambertz was also required reading. I lost count of how many times I completed it. At 10:00 the professed sisters would join us in the novitiate and someone would read from the Catholic newspaper, *The Tablet,* or a Catholic magazine, and after that, we'd have choir practice in the Chapel. We had to learn Gregorian chant. At first this was difficult, and I didn't like it. As a novice I would be required to chant the office every morning, which meant we had to learn Latin. I had had two years of high school Latin which helped with pronunciation, but I still had a lot of vocabulary to master. We would have dinner at noon. This was confusing because we would have dinner at lunchtime, and supper at dinnertime, very different from home. I would march into the refectory in rank and stand behind my chair with my hands folded. After Grace was said everyone walked in rank to a table where a novice would ladle the soup. There would be a short reading while we ate our soup and then the bell would ring for the end of silence. The soup bowls would be collected and the novices would begin serving the meal at the head table first. We would talk through coffee and dessert then back to the chapel for after dinner prayers. At last we were free for the afternoon. Sometimes the postulants with the Novice Mistress and the Assistant would take long walks, two by two, to the Patchogue Bay or around the residential area past the parish church, Our Lady of the Snow. We would talk and laugh. It was refreshing to get out and about. I'm sure to passers-by we looked like a picture taken from the children's book *Madeline*. When we got back to the convent, there was time to write the required letter home or study or read before Vespers.

Most people, including most Catholics use the word "sister" and "nun" interchangeably as I am doing. But in Church law they are quite distinct. Major differences can be found in the vows, work, and prayer life of each. Nuns take four vows: poverty, chastity, obedience and closure or stability. A nun lives a cloistered and contemplative life. They cannot legally own anything. They are not apostolic, which means they don't teach, nurse or work with people in any way except for the porter whose duty is to answer the door. The general public is familiar with a few examples. St. Thérèse of Lisieux also called the Little Flower made the Carmelite Order famous in the 1890s. More recently in the United States in the 1960s, Thomas Merton made the Trappists at Gethsemani, Kentucky well known through his books. The monastic communities must be self-sustaining financially so they make and sell jelly, bread, cheese, and wine or run retreat houses and some even raise and sell German Shepherds. And when they are not working, they are praying – morning, noon and night.

The prayer day is divided up into the Liturgy of the Hours also called the Breviary or Divine Office. It is the public prayer life of the Church. All deacons and priests must say it every day, as do those living in monasteries. It is made up of psalms, hymns and readings from the Bible. These together with the celebration of the Liturgy or Holy Mass, follows a yearly cyclical calendar marking the major liturgical events of Christmas and Easter, and the minor feast days of the Blessed Mother and the saints. In cloisters, the members rise during the night and chant Matins. Lauds is said at sunrise and Prime and Terce would be said midmorning. Sext would be said midday, None in mid-afternoon, Vespers in the evening and Compline at nightfall.

Semi-cloistered religious, like the Ursulines, are called sisters and they take the three vows of poverty, chastity and obedience but not closure. They can legally inherit property but not dispose of it. Because their work is apostolic it requires interaction with people whether in schools or hospitals, or wherever their mission takes them. The daily work is prayer in action and the sister tries to remain in the presence of God while she completes whatever assignment she is given. Apostolic sisters do not rise in the middle of the night to pray, but they are required to pray the hours during the day. When they are stationed in the houses, time constraints do not permit the chanting of the office. But in the novitiate young women are being formed to the ideal, so the day begins with the chanting of Matins and Lauds before Mass followed by a half hour of meditation. We recited Prime and Terce after breakfast and Sext and None after dinner at noon. Vespers was chanted at 4 P.M. and Compline was chanted at 8 P.M. right before going to bed. The Great Silence started after that and lasted until after Mass the next day. Only an emergency permitted this rule to be broken. Of course, one was always allowed to approach a Superior with a serious problem. It took postulants almost the entire year to learn all of this.

Every Sunday at the allotted time we wrote home. It was a requirement. We needed permission to write to grandparents or siblings, but that was never denied. A postulant or novice working on detachment didn't ask to write to friends. So for six years, I wrote only one letter a year to my best friend, Joan, who had joined the Sisters of Mercy in New Jersey, and then only at Christmas. My mother saved all of my letters home, more than a hundred over the course of nine years, and they have provided details that would have been long forgotten otherwise. I have read the collection a few times. The first time, I blushed with embarrassment at the childish, insipid, sentences. The next time, I wept at how devoid of feeling they were. Finally, I read them for the events and facts that punctuated the innocuous missives home. Like a red hot poker they have stoked the coals of memory and prodded them into bright bursts of recall. Thanks to my mother, they have become an invaluable resource in writing this memoir.

45

Letters home were left unsealed on the desk of the Novice Mistress. Incoming letters were delivered opened. None of them may have been read, but we didn't know that. Like soldiers forbidden to relay to loved ones information that could be used by the enemy, we knew instinctively that we were not to divulge the whereabouts of our emotions. I didn't really need to be told not to write negatively about the convent life I was living. My mother, years earlier, had prepared me to always paint the Church in pastels.

I wrote to my parents September 27, 1959:

> *Betty Martin sent me a nice picture of Joan, Pat,*
> *Gladys and Betty taken on Reception Day at the*
> *Mount. She would like one of the pictures you took*
> *of me. If you do send her a picture, please tell her*
> *how grateful I am for her thinking of me.*

And three months after I entered I wrote: *It still surprises me that Betty writes. I think I have gotten three or four letters from her.* Because she was not family, I never wrote back to Betty. I appreciated her tenacity in trying to keep in touch with a friend who could return nothing. She actually came to visit me the following July with Jerry, her future husband. I appreciated that too. My two grandmothers wrote to me from time to time, as did my brother and my dad. But my mother wrote only once or twice. That the privacy of her letters would be violated was more than she could endure. But it was just another example of "Sister says." Access to the events of the outside world was strictly controlled for those in training. We did not listen to the radio or watch television or even read the newspaper. We lined the garbage pails with newspapers but it was considered a fault to read them; so I didn't.

Of course we were kept abreast of big news. I wrote home in February, 1961:

> *We were very fortunate to see Eisenhower's Farewell*
> *Speech, the Inauguration and the State of the Un-*

ion Message on television. It was very interesting. We saw a good part of the parade too, but we didn't stay up for the ball, ha! I'm sure you know all about Jacqueline by now, Mom remember the Queen! Those news commentators spare no one and nothing...

I was always trying to engage my mother, hoping I suppose, that she would write back. In this letter I am referring to a family event that happened when I was in high school and we were visiting my brother in seminary. Queen Elizabeth on a state visit to Washington, DC waved to us from her limousine and we waved back. It was silly and the source of many jokes. I was also trying to reassure my mother that I wasn't totally deprived and got to watch TV from time to time. In the same letter I mention that my friends have written... *I heard from Gladys again. Between Gladys and Joan V... I'm kept up on the latest events.* This I thought was extraordinary since I never wrote back.

Mother Ursula would never let her sisters miss the election of the first Catholic President of the United States, John Fitzgerald Kennedy. It was our prayers that got him in, for heaven's sake! The news blackout on his extramarital exploits was a kindness, for Catholics at least.

Besides writing home on Sundays, the postulants spent time in the Chapel learning how to chant. Soon after I entered the order, the community changed from saying the Little Office of the Blessed Mother to the Divine Office said by priests. Only months before we had been teenagers shouting cheerleading chants at high school games; now we had to wrap our energies around Latin and Gregorian chant. It was going to be difficult, and I wrote home ... *Reverend Mother said she was going to have a Benedictine come in to show us how to chant* ... but I don't actually remember that happening. So Latin became a big deal even though I had studied it in high school. I didn't like Gregorian chanting at first. How do you go from *A Whole Lot of Shakin Going On* to a reduced antagonistic tonal scale of music? It takes time. But if there is one thing a postulant and novice has is time. A large part of the plainchant melodies were composed before the year 600 AD. The chant is named after

47

Gregory the Great who lived from 590 to 609 AD. Gregorian chant grew on me until it finally became soothing and pleasurable and another way to pray.

But we didn't just learn music written over 1500 years ago. Postulants and novices were always putting on little musical shows. This activity kept us busy and provided fun and entertainment for the older sisters as well. I loved it. We also enjoyed Saint's feast days and special visiting days when the routine changed and the rules were relaxed a bit. For instance in October 1959, Mother Germaine, the Mother General of the whole order who lived in Belgium, came to visit us in Blue Point. So besides polishing an already spotless convent, we had to prepare a show. I wrote home:

> *The novices did a gypsy number, tambourines and all. We Postulants did a Scotch drill. We had red and green tams made out of crepe paper. They were cute. The day before was a day of silence in preparation for the feast but on the 21st we had a free day. No work! No classes! And we can talk all day. Mother General brought a filmstrip of the Congo with her. She visited there last year. There were shots of the Prince Albert reservation – elephants, antelopes etc. The sisters in the Congo wear white habits. They really look nice.*

We had other things to distract us from the daily routine. A Hungarian sister called Mother Paula from Brazil came to spend time with us at Blue Point. Her community was disbanded so she could attach herself to any community that would have her. I don't know what brought her to Blue Point. I was taken with her plight, and I really thought it would be exciting to follow her back to Brazil or wherever her ministry took her. The old flames of being a missionary were easily ignited. But our Mother Vicar would never allow this charming, charismatic Hungarian nun to lure away one of her sisters. Soon the two women paid a visit to Bishop Fulton J. Sheen in New York City and came back with $500 for the cause, whatever that was. Bishop Sheen was a TV personality in the 1950s. It is still possible to buy a tape or DVD of his programs. When I went to Star of the Sea Grammar School in Long Branch, all the students were assigned to watch him for homework. He had a half hour show on Thursday evenings. He'd walk on stage and swirl his red cloak about him like Loretta Young twirling onto the stage. With a twinkle in his eye he instructed make-believe angels to wipe his black board. It would seem he was also generous to nuns in distress. The Hungarian nun left Blue Point, and I never heard about her again.

Postulants had to learn how to read in front of the community during meals. This created a great deal of anxiety for a shy person like me, even though I had spent so much time in Forensics giving speeches. In the beginning, we would be told to go up to the lectern and finish the reading started by a novice. In November, 1959 I wrote home:

> *Thursday I'll read for the whole dinner. Up until this time I've just replaced a novice for maybe five minutes (which seemed like hours) when you start it's all you can do to catch your breath. But then once I get started I have a tendency to race, which is silly because I'll only have to read more. Sometimes you don't even know when you've come to the end of a sentence and your voice is left hanging in the air. All this is funny in retrospect only.*

What I didn't tell my parents was that the fear of reading in the refectory was compounded by the knowledge that if I made any kind of mistake, I had to ask forgiveness of the superior afterwards. If I stumbled over a difficult word or skipped part of a sentence, I would go to the side of the seated Superior, when I was finished the reading, kneel down and ask forgiveness. She would accept that, and I red faced, would take my seat before we left for the chapel. I saw the novices do that as well. In addition, they went to the middle of the refectory floor and knelt down with outstretched arms and said a silent penance. These practices were designed to provide exercises in humility.

Every day there was something new to learn. We had to learn how to meditate. Some of us were acquainted with the word and had managed to sit quietly in the presence of God for modest amounts of time during the Exposition of the Blessed Sacrament, for example. But to do so for thirty minutes each morning before Mass required some initiation and training. In the beginning, just concentrating on a simple thought was enough, but eventually the goal was to empty your mind of all thoughts and worries and allow God's presence to enter your soul. There were levels of meditation and with God's grace and personal perseverance, humility and mortification you might be invited to more intimate levels of mysticism like the great saints. This was considered a lifetime endeavor.

Once a day the postulants met with the Novice Mistress both as a group and also privately. During the group sessions I began to take down a dictated explanation of the Holy Rule in my lined, bound copybook. When I had my personal meeting with Mother, I'd kneel beside her desk in the novitiate. It was a time for her to make comments and to ask questions. I also could ask questions or discuss my spiritual progress. This was also the time to ask for permissions. If I had run out of personal care items like soap or other personal products, I would ask permission to have more. Pads not tampons were available. But I knew some sisters did use tampons because when I was in 6th grade in Long Branch a sister gave me money to pick up a box for her on my way to school. I hardly needed to be asked to keep such an embarrassing task to myself. In our community you asked permission to lie down if you had a headache or cramps. You asked permission for aspirin. You asked permission to go to the doctor or dentist. You asked permission to stay home from school. And you had to ask permission to do a private penance. Once I asked for permission to put a small stone in my shoe for a specific amount of time. I don't remember my motivation, nor do I remember asking to do it again. However, virtually nothing was done in the convent without the permission of the superior.

Intimate conversations with other postulants, novices, or professed sisters were forbidden. One postulant left during the course of the year, but it was never discussed. Of course as I learned more and more of what it meant to take vows and what it meant to live the life of a religious, I had doubts and I presumed others did too. Whenever I became homesick, I thought about leaving and for me that usually happened in late afternoon. But the next day I would dismiss my feelings as temptations to be overcome. We were allowed to discuss this with the Novice Mistress but not with one another. An older second year novice was assigned to each postulant to teach her how to do the chores of the house, but she was not supposed to become a confidant; however, mine became a good friend for life. I was driven to do everything perfectly, because that's what I thought I was supposed to do. One afternoon, Sr. Ruth Henry was showing me how to scrub the guest parlor floor. I must have been visibly agitated. She showed me that I didn't need to scrub off the design in the tile, that God only wanted me to do my reasonable best. She always showed the middle way with gentleness and humor.

Since all the chores or charges rotated, it eventually became my turn to serve in the refectory. I dreaded this more than reading. The only former experience I'd had as a waitress was at Riverview Hospital in a volunteer breakfast position. I would approach a handsome doctor and take his order for coffee and pastry. But by the time I walked the ten steps to the kitchen area, I couldn't remember if he wanted it black or with sugar. Was it a doughnut or toast? I was too shy and embarrassed to go back and make it right. So I'd stage whisper to my friend Joan, "Go ask him if he wants milk in his coffee." She would reluctantly go out and retake his order. I was soon encouraged to quit because you can't fire a volunteer.

There were no menus or orders taken in the refectory, but it wasn't going to be easy either. I wrote home on January 18, 1960:

> *I finally got through the week of serving without any mishaps. But on second thought the first time I was asked to take a tray downstairs (and of course told to be careful) I broke a dish or if you will it slipped off the top (no, I didn't get any glass in the food, Mom, ha!) You know how I pour, well I didn't spill anything but I did almost scorch the tip of somebody's ear with the side of the teapot...)*

I am trying to be funny. Besides being readers, members of my family were all amateur humorists in the tradition of Mark Twain who was nearly revered as a saint by my father. But the reference to getting something in the food was not really funny. My mother suffered from obsessive-compulsive disorder. Once when making a cake to donate for a fundraiser, my dad opened a can of beer near the bowl. My mother, worried that droplets of alcohol had contaminated the batch, threw it out and started over. Years later, she told me the OCD began after we moved to Long Branch. She had library books on the kitchen table and began to worry that her coffee had somehow damaged them. The focus of her obsession might be on religion or money or hand washing. This disorder caused her endless suffering and embarrassment and significantly contributed to her depression.

My parents braved the Long Island Expressway, more appropriately called the LIE, nearly every month for a visit. They deserved a medal of some kind. If it was nice outside, we sat in the garden; if not, we sat in the parlor. Superiors and older professed sisters would wander among the chatting families and often sit and join in. There would be no heart to hearts in the parlor. Parents and guests would be invited to the guest dining room (with the scrubbed and polished floor) where they'd be given refreshments. We weren't permitted to sit or eat with them. This really annoyed my mother. After a couple of hours, they would make the long ride home. In February I wrote:

> *It doesn't really make any difference to me so you do what works out best at your end but next visiting day would probably be the best time for Mary Jane and Joan to come out. Emily works with Joan and might like to come out with them but that might be too much of a squeeze.*

My high school friends had not forgotten me but it was so difficult for them to make the long trip. Mary Jane and Joan were able to come up with my parents but there was not enough room for Emily. I appreciated their loyalty.

Parents were still expected to pay for certain expenses. In April, 1960 I wrote:

You said you wanted to get me something for Easter well...Would you be able to take care of the cape and a new pair of shoes. I think the cost of the cape is on the bill if not it's around $50. You know what shoes to get, don't you Mom?

Technically, the community wasn't responsible for us financially until we were clothed in the Ursuline habit. I certainly never even thought about medical insurance and my parents never asked about it. We didn't go to the dentist for regular teeth cleaning either. Only when my impacted wisdom teeth caused great pain did I ask to go to the dentist as a novice. Our postulant year went by quickly. We were still studying and taking exams in Math and Theology, but we were also getting ready to be invested or clothed in the habit. Our long black dresses were being made and fitted. I had taken a few lessons on my Singer sewing machine during senior year and Sr. Philip appreciated that little bit of expertise as she taught me how to cut and seam. We would soon dress exactly as the professed nuns except that we would wear white veils. Everyone would know that although we were molded and set to rise, like loaves of bread, we weren't yet baked in the heat of the oven.

In May, 1960 I wrote:

The most exciting happening however occurred Wednesday. We all tried on our new habits. Most of the postulants tried them on in the afternoon but it took so long that Ninita and I (the last two) were trying them on in the evening. The others were out pulling dandelions. Well I haven't been so silly in a long time. I wish you could have seen us. They really fit nice and they look nice too. But the sleeves weren't in yet when we put them on and I look just a wee bit awkward. Sr. Philip is so patient with us. You can imagine the work she has and then to try to fit seven silly postulants but she can't help laughing at us either...

———🙙🙙🙙———

I had arrived in September eager and excited to become a religious. Now nine months later, the waiting period was almost over. I had been instructed, and observed and tested. The superiors decided that I could continue on the path to becoming a Canonical novice. I would be given my religious name and I would don the habit of an Ursuline, but I would wear a white veil to let all know that I had not yet taken vows.

Clothing Day June 27, 1960

The guests were seated in the small chapel behind the community of sisters. My mom, dad, brother and Father Neumann filled a pew. I was dressed in a simple white wedding gown along with six other postulants. Walter P. Kellenberg, the Bishop of the Diocese of Rockville Centre sat in the sanctuary and Mother Ursula sat in front of the altar rail to the right. The postulants were asked their intentions one by one, and I replied that I wanted to take the veil of an Ursuline. The black habits were blessed and handed to each of us. We exited the chapel to change; then processed back in again dressed in our new black robes, with a large rosary hanging from the knotted cincture around our waists. One by one, we knelt in front of the Bishop to receive our new name in religion, and then knelt in front of Mother Vicar to receive her blessing as well. I would now be called Sister Mary Christine of Jesus and Mary. A white crown of flowers was placed on my head. The community welcomed each of us as we processed out of the chapel. Our picture was taken in front of the Motherhouse with the Bishop and the Reverend Mother Vicar and the Bishop's assistant, Father McGann. Pictures were taken with the families in the garden and refreshments were provided the guests in the dining room.

Sr.Walter, Sr.Domenica, Sr. Agnus Dei, Sr.Angelus, Bishop Kellenburg, Sr. Amadeus, Sr. Aloyisius, Sr.Christine, Mother Ursula, Father McGann Blue Point, NY, 1960

Finally I looked like a nun. But I was still a nun in the making – a canonical novice. I could add the letters RU after my name, which stood for the French, Religieux Ursuline. I felt happy that as a bride of Christ I was fortunate to have his name as part of my own. I was ecstatic. I had fallen in love with God. I glowed. I was eighteen.

I gave my parents and brother a hug and waved good-by to the Father. They got into their cars and returned to New Jersey. I returned to the hard work of being a first year novice that meant devoting myself entirely to formation and training in the life of the community. Like all canonical novices I was not permitted to work outside the convent, even to teach the weekly catechism lessons to the children. I was entering into an intense period of training governed by Church law.

William Bassler and Sr. Christine, RU Clothing Day June 27, 1960

That evening I had supper and said my prayers as usual. I was not looking forward to what was going to happen before we went to bed. A few second year novices came to the bathroom to cut our hair. I knew it wasn't going to be shaved off as outsiders believed. My hair was never my crowning glory. My wisps wouldn't fill a fairy's pincushion. I was happy to cover it up with the headdress of an Ursuline. Still for me, it was a meaningful act of submission. I sat resigned and offered it up to my Spouse, Jesus Christ. No tears. No outward demonstration of my inner thoughts. But I resented the young novice who manifested a perverse glee in lifting my hair and cutting it off. New recruits in the armed services do have their heads shaved. There are lots of reasons. It subdues personality. It eliminates originality. It is practical hygiene. Also, a young woman, especially years ago, would think twice before impulsively bolting out of the convent with a close-cropped head. As canonical novices, we were entering the basic training of religious life, a Marine's Paris Island, if you will. But first, I did experience a honeymoon phase.

The next morning my heart filled with a happiness difficult to describe. I walked on air. I was in love. I kissed each article of clothing while I dressed and recited the appropriate prayers. We had moved out of our postulant rooms into the novices' cubicles. These were smaller, windowless spaces, with a curtain across the front. But as far as I was concerned my cubicle was elegant and fit for a bride of Christ. *The Song of Solomon* is often used to capture the longing of the soul for intimacy with the mystical bridegroom: "By night on my bed I sought him whom my soul loveth…"

The English word " mortification" comes from the Latin *mortificare* which means to kill, to subdue. The idea of mortifying the flesh goes back to the desert fathers who lived 200 to 300 years after the death of Jesus. Some of the ideas of desert monasticism about the body, the soul, sex and pleasure persist to this day. Their philosophy, put most simply, is if it feels good then it must be evil; and if it hurts then it must be good. Their attitudes toward women became misogynistic. Their thinking still colors current Church teachings.

We might say we're mortified to walk across a stage or we're mortified to be seen buying something in a second hand store. But it also means to overcome the demands of the body and its desires and feelings through pain and by doing without things. As postulants we were made aware that the life of a sister was one of mortification. We were going to be giving up lots of things and material comforts. We were going to cut our hair and wear a long black habit in hot summers without complaining. We knew the life of a religious was one of discipline. But we weren't told about *the discipline* until we became novices.

One of the first things the new novices did at recreation was to make our own disciplines. We sat chatting while we wove from heavy cotton twine a little whip. It had five strands that were braided into a handle. The five strands were to remind us of the five wounds of our crucified Savior. Each strand had a few knots tied along it and at the tip. It was a private act of devotion to be done on Fridays for the duration of the Our Father. We went to our cubicles and got ready for bed. At the signal, we lifted our nightgowns and began to whip our left hip. Because the panels separating our cubicles were thin you could hear the seven of us whipping our bodies. Some, as I recall, were pretty loud. At the end of the Our Father we all stopped. One was forbidden to use it more often without permission from the Superior.

I wrote in my copybook as dictated:

> *The common life is based on mortification. A mortified person is a happy one and an unmortified person is not for she is a slave of her passions. Happiness and advancement in virtue are also found in the renouncement of self. Our penances consist usually in the following, eating five minutes standing at breakfast and praying three Hail Mary's, the discipline is taken once a week except in Lent when it is taken twice. Let us perform this penance in a spirit of humility uniting it with the scourging of Our Lord. We must however use it with discretion.*

Of course I had mixed feelings about this practice. Part of me thought it was creepy like some of the stranger *Lives of the Saints* we had been reading in the refectory. Simeon Stylites, who spent his life on a raised pillar, comes to mind. Part of me thought it seemed the right thing to do as a nun trying to be holy. I presumed the Second Vatican Council did away with these medieval practices until I read Mary Johnson's 2012 memoir, *An Unquenchable Thirst.* I learned not only do the Missionaries of Charity founded by Mother Teresa of Calcutta in 1950 still use the discipline; they also wear a spiked wire chain on their arm and around their waist for certain periods of the day. As I said at the outset, the more things change, the more they stay the same.

We were now students of the Holy Rule. A Holy Rule is a document that you use to evaluate how you are measuring up to the religious life, similar to a 12-inch school ruler. "Rules" have been written by different founders of religious orders and communities. St. Angela de Merici founded the Ursulines in 1535 in Italy. Her idea was simplicity itself. A group of women would live at home but meet for prayer and devote themselves to good works. They opened orphanages and schools. Neither she nor they considered themselves "nuns." Her idea spread quickly throughout Italy, Germany and France. St. Angela died in 1540. It took only forty years for a man, a certain Bishop Charles Borromeo, to completely subvert the Saint's brilliant grass roots movement. After I told my mother I was going to enter the convent, she would often lament: "Can't you do good works at home?" St. Angela would have answered: "Yes!" However, a Bishop would have much more control if he encouraged the women to take vows of poverty, chastity, and obedience, to wear a habit, to become a religious congregation of women, and to be enclosed in a community. Bishop Borromeo declared the group of women a religious order under the ancient Rule of St. Augustine. St. Augustine who lived in the 4th century had been asked to resolve a conflict among the nuns in a monastery that had been ruled by his sister and where his cousin and niece lived. So he wrote letters that outlined how he thought religious women should conduct themselves. It became known as the Rule of St. Augustine. Almost three hundred years later in 1818 Reverend John Lambertz of Tildonk,

Belgium founded a new branch of Ursulines called the Ursulines of Tildonk who would continue to follow the Rule of St. Augustine but with new Constitutions to govern them.

We seven recently veiled and clothed novices were each given a personal copy. The Rule never changes but the Constitutions can and are rewritten from time to time. Pope John XXIII called on communities to reexamine them in the light of *aggiornamento* which means "bringing up to date." The word came to embody the spirit of renewal sweeping the church.

The Rule itself is pretty straightforward, but just so everyone would interpret the Rule more or less the same, it was felt that an Explanation of the Holy Rule was needed. The canonical novices met every day with the Novice Mistress and copied by hand into two leather bound copybooks extensive interpolations of the Rule. I don't know who compiled the stories and examples used to teach us how to be Ursulines, or even how old they were. Some were timeless bits of wisdom of how to live peaceably with many women from different backgrounds. Others were dated, wacky anecdotes, European, and alien to young American women. I include rather long excerpts from my copybooks to demonstrate the relentless education that took place daily to transform the behavior of a lay-woman or rather a teenager into the stereotypical behavior of a sister.

On page 27 I write:

If we do not take care, our talents will leave us a longer time in purgatory than if we had not had them. For probably without them we would be more humble. Let us remember Luther. As a novice great things were foretold of him. He was so exact so fervent and yet later on he defied the Pope and is now the father of millions of Protestants. It was through pride that he failed. The honor of publishing Indulgences had not been given to his Order and his pride revolted and yet for years he had been a model religious.

I was so glad I had never told anyone that my great-grandfather was a Lutheran minister. Actually he functioned as a Bishop in the English Evangelical Lutheran Church of Western Pennsylvania from the 1840s through the Civil War – founding schools, orphanages and churches. According to records, when he was only four years old, he emigrated with his father, Franz, from Langenthal, Canton Bern, Switzerland. His mother and sibling died aboard ship. At fifty-four he died of tuberculosis. Only one of his seven children lived to become my grandfather, William. Rev. Gottlieb and Eliza are probably the most saintly people in my family tree.

On page 54, the exhortations on how to conduct oneself as a nun continue:

> *We must be extremely careful in the modesty of our looks. The majority of our faults begin by a look then follows a thought then the desire then the consent. Saint Aloysius though a courtier at the Spanish court had never seen the queen's face. Saint John Berchmans was so modest that it was said of him that should the rule of Saint Ignatius get lost it could easily be found in Berchman's conduct.*

> *-Never stare at a person...*

> *-We must not read what falls under our observation...*

> *-We must be like lakes between our sisters...*

> *-The word "why" is not included in the dictionary of a religious...*

> *- We should be like brooms in the hands of our Superior. We use a broom and then put it away until we need it again. Our Superiors should be able to do the same with us. A broom does not murmur or find fault if we use it or not...*

-Let us rejoice for we are on the good road which leads to heaven

-We should throw ourselves on it like a cannon ball.

-Let us never carry tales. Some people are like telegrams.

And so forth and so on. I didn't laugh or question what I was writing. These admonitions were being presented so that I would imitate them. I realized that the mountain to perfection had way more than seven stories for me to climb, all due respect to Thomas Merton.

And how would the new recruits for Jesus whip themselves into shape? The key to the new deployment was called Chapter. It was a pause in the afternoon, when all the novices assembled in the novitiate to accuse themselves of whatever faults they had committed during the past twenty-four hours. We had written down the examples of perfection in our copybook and now we judged ourselves accordingly. What in secular life would not have been given a second thought in religious life was put under a microscope and deemed a failing. For example, had you questioned your Superior even in your thoughts? Or had you read the newspaper as you lined the garbage pails? Had you spoken more than was necessary during chores? As a postulant I had been excused from this exercise, but as a novice I soon learned that my history teacher had been right after all. I was living most of the memorable scenes in *The Nun's Story*. Only I wasn't Audrey Hepburn and Blue Point was most assuredly not Hollywood.

The Novice Mistress sat at her desk and the assembled novices sat at the outside of the tables in rank forming a large U. Each novice took her turn and walked to the center of the room and knelt down. She did not have the option of taking a pass. To assume perfection, after all, would have violated the essence of humility. So she accused herself of whatever faults she thought she had committed whether they had been witnessed or not. Of course, if she accused herself of talking during the Great Silence then that left open the question, whom did she talk to? What could the other party do, but accuse herself of doing the same thing? "J'aime accuse..." These offences were of course not "sins" in the Catechism sense but the new refined "sins" of the convent world. Punishments would be given nonetheless. A simple penance might be praying in the Chapel with arms outstretched for the space of three Hail Marys. If the offense was deemed serious enough, then the sister would be given a penance to be served during mealtime. So someone might be given the punishment of eating their breakfast on their knees in the middle of the refectory. This was initially very embarrassing and for me, it never got easy. There was usually no talking during breakfast and the whole thing was over relatively quickly. But some breakfasts were easier to eat on your knees than others. Soft-boiled eggs were tricky, especially if the sister in charge got distracted, and removed them from the water before three minutes had passed. I was glad I had learned how to crack and eat them in Mrs. Dowd's kitchen years before.

A really serious offense like talking during the Great Silence or a serious disobedience like walking in the garden with a two-some instead of a threesome could be punished by having the sister eat her whole dinner in the middle of the refectory. We were warned against particular friendships between ourselves and our future students. So any infraction related in any way to this prohibition resulted in a much longer penance and everybody knew you had done something very wrong. On the other hand, animosities between sisters were also greatly discouraged. If I had had cross-words with another sister, I would have to seek her out later and get on my knees and beg forgiveness. Thinking back on it now, if I include prayer time, I probably spent 45% of my day on my knees.

Also, if I dropped food on my serviette while I was eating, I had to go out to the middle of the refectory and accuse myself of that fact. My appetite suffered and I lost weight. So much so, that my mother who was terrified of nuns and priests, nonetheless, sent a letter to Mother Vicar stating her concern about my weight loss.

Mother Vicar, who didn't want to lose a novice, wrote back to my mother and my mother saved the letter.

Oct 3, 1960

Dear Mrs. Basseler

I am sure you would like a word of assurance about your dear daughter. Rest assured that she is in the best of health. She is very happy. I agree with you she has lost a little weight but as she tells me, she was too heavy when she entered. I took her to a good specialist who gave her a thorough examination and he found her in perfect health. However, on my asking he prescribed some vitamins for her. Sister Christine is really very happy, dear Mrs. Basseler, and I do not think you have any need to worry. I quite understand you, dear Mrs. Basseler, and I was very happy to accede to your demand. With all best wishes from the Sisters, and assuring you and Mr. Basseler of a very special remembrance in our prayers. Very sincerely in Christ.

This letter is not signed and "Bassler" is misspelled four times. My mother had gone to bat for me a second time; and again, I didn't know it. What I did know was that I now got an eggnog before breakfast, and wine and cheese before going to bed. An unseen hand placed it on the butler's window in the refectory and I stood by myself in the large empty room taking a sip of red wine. God's will be done. I really don't remember the vitamins.

———※———

There were many charges or jobs necessary to keep a large motherhouse in order, and mercifully they rotated. Of course, the bathrooms and dorms had to be cleaned daily. The guest parlors were kept immaculate in case a Father or the Bishop dropped by unexpectedly. The stairs had to be swept down with a brush and dustpan every day. The halls had to be swept with compound and then buffed with a large electric buffer. Institutional wax has a very distinctive smell, not unpleasant just distinctive. Studies on the sense of smell are ongoing but difficult to quantify. Researchers suspect it may be more powerful than all the other senses. I have walked down the corridor of an old building and have been immediately transported back to my days as a novice because of the smell of waxed buffed floors.

Laundry was done by the novices and postulants. The large industrial washing machines could handle the sheets and dirty clothes of forty women. Spinners got the wash damp dry . Then it all had to be carried outside and hung up. In the winter everything would be taken off the line frozen and then splayed out on the folding tables to finish drying. The sheets were put through a large mangle. But the bandeaux had to be starched and ironed stiff. If you look closely at a picture, the bandeau was a piece of linen that each sister could fold to fit her forehead. It had two strings that tied at the back of the head. The veil could then be draped over it and pinned to the side of the bonnet and also pinned at the back of the neck. Everything would be folded and sorted according to the number sewn on the clothing. Everyone helped on laundry day.

Sisters could be assigned to working the "bread cage." This was in a different part of the cellar. It was a large walk-in-cage with cupboards to hold the loaves of bread delivered daily. The cage perhaps was designed for another use because it wasn't fine enough to keep out rodents and we didn't have dogs or cats. During charge time, two sisters would go down twice a day and slice the bread for meals. This was an exception to the rule forbidding two sisters to walk together in the garden, for example. Not everyone could cut the bread into reasonably even slices. If your work was too awful, you'd be reprimanded and that gave you something to accuse yourself of in Chapter later that day for which you'd receive a penance. You had to estimate how much bread to slice in the first place. Not enough was a sure disaster. But if too much was left over that meant stale bread in the morning and no one wanted that. After meals, the novices in charge would wrap up the bread that was not used. What was needed for the next day was reported to Sr. Joseph, a professed sister who actually did the ordering over the phone.

Once when my parents were visiting, the Novice Mistress called me from the garden to the bread cage and pointed out what I had done wrong. I knelt, accepted the reprimand and returned to my visit without pouting. Of course I would not mention to my parents what had happened. All for Jesus. I was proud of myself that I'd been able to do that without crying which is what I felt like doing. But I resented it nonetheless. This was all part of the discipline and training in obedience and humility. When I watch a drill sergeant scream in the face of a recruit, I know the recruit knows he's being conditioned, but it is still difficult. I mentioned earlier that I was naturally pliant and wanted to please; but this aspect of my personality was being sorely tested. Paradoxically, I was also naturally argumentative and strong willed. My father in particular did not think I'd last in the convent because of this trait. In the 1970's, after I left the convent, I laughed with my parents at Archie Bunker yelling at his wife, "Stifle yourself Edith." But while I was a nun, I had to stifle myself on an hourly basis.

Taking care of the chapel was another chore. It was a coveted charge to be in the presence of the Eucharistic Christ in the tabernacle. But it had great responsibilities; and so although it was physically an easy charge, it could be nerve wracking for a careful person. Father's vestments had to be laid out just so. The water and wine prepared just so. The ribbon marker placed in the Missal just so. In a July, 1960 letter I told my parents: *Everyone is assigned different charges for the summer and I'm on the Chapel charge. I'm just lucky I guess...*

Food preparation was a daily time consuming task. The novices learned how to cook institutional style under the tutelage of a professed nun, Sister Joseph. We learned how to make mashed potatoes for forty people in an industrial mixer. We learned how to prepare and place the veal patties in cast aluminum pans and cook them. Those in charge of breakfast were way ahead of any fast food restaurant. In fifteen minutes or less, the time it takes to say a rosary, four novices would pour the orange juice and milk, prepare coffee and tea. Place the cereal boxes on platters, put out the

66

bread and butter, heat up the precooked bacon, and cook the eggs. These were usually soft-boiled eggs that were served in little aluminum cups. As mentioned before, timing was crucial; otherwise they were a runny mess. Sometimes we had baked eggs with cheese and they were served in oval cast aluminum pans.

We were always served good food. But I must mention the downside of sitting in rank for those at the end of the table; especially on the days we had boxed cereal. The older professed sisters sat at the top of the table with Mother Vicar at the head. They chose respectable boxes of cornflakes or rice puffs. So by the time the platter reached me the only choice left was Fruit-Loops. Fruit-Loops are cheerio-like circles of blue, pink, orange and red which turn milk into swirls of color. They looked awful and tasted awful... now and forever, Amen. At ten o'clock in the morning we had a snack break and in the afternoon we had a tea break. As students we were exempt from the Lenten fast, so although I didn't gain weight I was never hungry.

Mother Ursula kept a bird to which she fed Belgian endive. So every so often a box of endive would arrive from Europe. When there were enough for all of us, we would prepare a special dish. The novices learned how to trim and cut a cross in the bottoms of the endive. They would then be poached lightly and wrapped in thin ham slices and placed in the oval aluminum pans. A cheese sauce would be prepared to cover the endives and they would be baked. This dish was served with mashed potatoes. The delicious combination of ham and cheese disguised the bitter flavor of the endive, which was a slowly acquired taste. It has become a tradition in my home to serve this on Christmas Eve.

Some afternoons the entire novitiate sat down together to peel potatoes. We sat at a long table in the basement, while someone read. At home I had peeled potatoes under running water, but now I peeled them dry and I found it very unpleasant. The acrid smell of damp peelings soaked into my pores and stayed there even after washing my hands. But all work and no play makes even novices cranky. So we did play. On nice days we played baseball. Sometimes we played badminton. Laughter broke out over the most childish things and was infectious. We could be very silly. My Grandmother Kerr would have said we were high-spirited.

I mentioned earlier our musical and dramatic presentations for the older sisters. We did productions for all kinds on feast days and holidays. In 1960 I wrote home telling my parents:

> *...the next thing will be the Easter play. It's about Christ before Pilate. I'll give you one guess who got the part of Pilate – type casting of course- that's right, yours truly, Laurence Olivier. Reminded me of when I was in second grade and got the part of the witch in Hansel and Gretel. I have a deep voice, I guess.*

Later in the summer of 1960 I wrote:

> *We started the summer schedule yesterday. We get up at quarter to six. Vespers and Dinner are earlier. Our group is taking English lessons from Sister Imelda in the morning. In the evening all the novices have a lesson in teaching catechism. I like that. We're excited about teaching next year and there is so much to know...We go at four thirty to starch and iron the bandeaux. It is 25 after now.*

The community owned an old Victorian house on the bay that gave us a private place to swim. And even though this was a strict semi-cloistered convent, the postulants and novices had swimsuits. During the summer we would pile into cars and drive the couple of miles to Bayport for an afternoon swim. That made my mother feel good because she knew how much I loved to swim. We brought bathing suits from home; so even if a boat happened by, we looked like young women enjoying the afternoon on the beach. We could write letters or read or talk or swim or lie out in the sun. This was a real treat. The house had an old piano and I often played duets with another sister. I wrote home in the summer of 1960:

We were at the bay and there were tiny, little fish swimming in and around the rocks. Sr. Domenica and myself decided to try and catch one of them in a bathing cap. We finally caught one. They're tricky little things. Well great was our surprise when another sister put him in her hand, and he started to blow up. Conclusion: we have baby Blowfish growing up in our bay. We had more fun though picking him up by his tail, he'd blow up then deflate. We'd give him a dunk and he'd do it all over again. Poor thing what an experience but he's back with the others now.

—◦◦◦—

We had Mother Ursula to thank for our summerhouse on the bay and for another beautiful piece of property on Long Island. They were bequeathed to the community. Mother Ursula would visit and befriend elderly women who in gratitude would will their estates to the community. As a professed Junior sister, I actually drove Mother Ursula to a nearby home and sat in the car while she had tea with, I suspect, a lonely lady who was probably a potential donor. I also remember a bedridden woman upstairs that the novices visited once in a great while. Perhaps she also traded her estate for lifetime care by the good sisters.

However, I knew very little about the woman who was my Superior to whom I made a solemn promise to obey. Once when I was in her office, she saw me staring at a picture on her desk. She told me it was taken when her parents were on safari. So I presumed she had come from money. Recently, I was told that her parents knew Sir Thomas Lipton who founded Lipton Tea. At the time, I didn't know that Mother Ursula was born Charlotte Tindrell in Glasgow in 1888 and was sent to a Belgium boarding school at Londerzeel run by the Ursulines. There she converted to Catholicism and later entered the convent where she had attended school. In time she became Headmistress of the girl's school. When her parents died, the strict rules of the semi-cloistered nuns were not waived and she was not given permission to return to England for their funerals. Once during evening recreation, she came in and began telling us the story of how she and a group of boarding school girls had to walk a great distance ahead of the advancing German troops in World War I. She had war experiences from World War II as well. Unfortunately, there never was enough time to hear the entire saga. Eventually in 1948, her Superior in Belgium, the Mother General of the global community ordered her to the United States to become the Vicar of the American sisters probably because she had leadership skills, was intelligent, and also spoke English. In the long run, this did not go well. Ursulines from Canada had started the Blue Point community in Ozone Park in 1924. Young women from Ireland were also recruited for the missions stateside. The community had schools in Connecticut and Long Island so American women from these schools were now also entering the ranks. Change can be treacherous. The Second Vatican Council opened windows, and then people didn't know what to do with the breeze. Religious communities had to respond. Because external trappings are easier to change than internal behaviors they are the first and easiest to address. The Belgium sisters had already greatly modified their habits. The veil was simplified and the skirts were shortened. When Mother Germaine came to visit us in 1965 she was wearing the modern habit. She saw what our "new" habits would look like, and she was not pleased. Mother Ursula who had the courage to outrun the Nazis was unable to outrun fashion and all it implied. The Irish sisters in particular had the ear of the Mother General, although the American sisters also felt the aging Vicar was too foreign. So in 1965 Mother Ursula was recalled to Belgium where she lived out her days. I had heard she requested a return to Blue Point but this was denied; however, a headstone marks her place in the Blue Point community cemetery. Mother Ursula died March 3, 1975 and was buried at Tildonk, Belgium.

I did participate in a burial at Blue Point as a novice. We had an older sister named Sr. Georgine whose job was to answer the front door. Her permanent chore was porter, and she was hard of hearing. She had the sweetest smile and spirit of anyone I've ever met. Everyone loved Sr. Georgine. Once when I was working in the kitchen getting supper ready, somebody said we were having popsicles for dessert. I let out a loud "Hot dog!" and Sr. Georgine got all excited because she thought we were having hot dogs for supper. Seven months later in 1961 I wrote home about this sweet soul.

> *Sr. Georgine got very sick in the morning and about 10 o'clock they took her to the hospital. She died Tuesday morning at 9 o'clock. It all happened so fast that everyone was stunned. I still miss her and Rev. Mother Vicar was heartbroken...Sr. Georgine was very holy even before she entered at the age of 48. She was a very exceptional person – please keep her in your prayers.*

Mother Ursula was visibly shaken by Sr. Georgine's death. It is fair to say she felt guilty that she hadn't taken Sr. Georgine to the doctor on Friday when she reported being ill. But we learned later that she died of meningitis. Considering the speed of her sickness and death, she might have had streptococcus pneumonia, which is deadly among the elderly. Her room was fumigated and kept empty for at least a year. Our parents were never notified. Sr. Georgine was buried in the community cemetery on the property, hers the only funeral I ever attended as a nun. But tragedy was soon to strike one of our own Canonical novices.

In the fall it was back to routine. I wrote on September 18, 1960... *I told you about Sr. Aloysius' mother before but I think she is slowly dying of cancer please keep her and the family in your prayers.* Only five months later I wrote home on February 11, 1961... *Sr. M Aloysius' mother died. Please keep the family in your prayers.*

When I was in second grade a little classmate became gravely ill. In third grade she died. All the girls in the class dressed in their First Communion dresses and attended her Funeral Mass and also went to the cemetery. I never forgot it. But now as Canonical novices we did not go to the wake or funeral or gravesite to be a comfort to our sister in religion. I do not recall, nor did I write home about any special marking of the passing of Sister Aloysius' mother, but this must have caused her great suffering, and it must have been a tremendous cross for her to bear so early in her religious life.

March meant spring cleaning, Lent, and Easter with visits from family. June was busy preparing for the Postulants' Clothing ceremony. We had another retreat week. In July my Grandmother Bassler came up for a visit. As much as she loved me, it must have been difficult for her to explain to her Lutheran friends that her granddaughter had become a nun. She wrote to me faithfully.

In the mornings we had English lessons with Sr. Joseph and in the evenings we had lessons on how to teach Catechism. In the afternoons we could go to the Bay for a swim. The summer went by quickly and soon we had served our Canonical year and became second year novices. As second year novices we were again allowed to "hit the books" and were now carrying seven college credits.

October 24, 1961 I wrote:

> *A lot of things have happened since the last time. We've been at classes for about a month now in fact next week we're having tests in English and Philosophy. So you'll really have to forgive me for not writing a lot. I really have to study. On Monday afternoon Mr. Artis comes to give us a two hr. class in Philosophy. Tuesday morning we have a two hr class with Fr. Mullin. Saturday morning we spend three hrs. With Sr. Alphonsus on English.*

I knew I was fortunate to be getting my education before I was sent out to teach in the schools. This was something else that Mother Ursula felt strongly about. I had a friend in the Sisters of Mercy in New Jersey who as a second year novice taught all day and went to college part time. Learning on the job it is called and it didn't help Anna Mae's self-confidence one bit. People don't expect a surgeon to start cutting before he's finished his studies, or a plumber to fix pipes before he's licensed; yet thousands of young women across the United States were sent into the classroom totally unprepared to teach 50 to 60 students in a class. It would be ironic, that the

Ursulines of Tildonk who were so medieval in some respects were so progressive in respect to teacher preparation, except that from the very beginning in Europe and the Americas the Ursuline name has been linked to quality education for young women.

—~(/)/~—

I was now beginning to prepare in earnest to take my first vows. A vow is a special, solemn, promise, a commitment for life. And even though in the United States, one out of two people divorce after taking marriage vows, it is safe to say that most people take them in good faith and with sincerity. After nearly three years of preparation, I was going to take vows of poverty, chastity and obedience. But I still wasn't absolutely sure if I could make this commitment for life.

Once, as a novice, I tried to talk to the priest in the confessional, which is not unlike talking to the IRS about your taxes. I told him I wanted to go home. He said I was tied to my mother's apron strings. I really couldn't deny that. I missed my family very much, and by late afternoon, loneliness would engulf me during Vespers. Quiet tears would stream down my face. The Novice Mistress was not insensitive to this but said later she thought I needed to work it through myself.

Our daily life proscribed constant examination of our deeds and motives: during the Confiteor at Mass, during Examin, during Chapter, at night before bed. I wrote in my copybook:

> *We have Chapter the guardian of order and humility an easy and efficacious means of doing away with our ordinary faults. We must assist at this exercise first with a firm desire of advancing our spiritual perfection, second to humble ourselves by accusing ourselves of the fault that will most humble us and accept generously any remark the Superior may make, thirdly unite our humiliations to those of our Lord and thereby increase our merit. Exteriorly one bends in accusing oneself but interiorly one should*

humiliate oneself in thinking that one is accusing
oneself out loud so that all may know we have failed
in this or that. The devil is no lover of Chapter.

And neither was I. The self-scrutiny was unrelenting. During one of my weekly chats with the Novice Mistress, I asked her if scrupulosity was necessary to become holy. She reassured me that it was not. Because my mother suffered from obsessive-compulsive behavior, which was currently focused on religious observance, I had reason to be worried. I didn't want to become scrupulous like my mother.

I continued to write in my copybook:

-Some novices have the good habit of taking a point
of exactitude which they have not yet acquired then
they take   another.

-Our Rule is read every Friday and it is a rule that
after having read it we examine our conduct.

-For example examination of conscience is a great
help.

-Before beginning each action let us ask ourselves for
whom and for what reason I am going to work-After
the work is finished   make a slight review and say
thank you Jesus, pardon for the faults and thank you
if I have done well.

And we also had periodic retreats spent in total silence except to speak to our Novice Mistress or the priest conducting the retreat. It was still more introspection in an already rarefied atmosphere, like being an orchid in an exotic hothouse. I rattled around in my own head until at the end of one of these spiritual marathons I began to think I WAS the Little Flower. I thought of St.Thérèse who died of tuberculosis when she was twenty-four and was canonized a saint in 1925. I still wanted to be a saint, but I didn't want to go crazy in the process.

I was also taking five college credits in Logic and Composition and Rhetoric, which demanded readings and papers along with this intense study of what was involved in taking the vows. Each vow was explained and dissected and analyzed and reflected upon over and over again.

This is what I copied about poverty:

A The vow of poverty forbids all rights of property

B All exercise of proprietorship

By the solemn vow of poverty both A and B are forbidden.

By the simple vow, which we take, B alone is forbidden. An Ursuline may inherit property but she cannot act as proprietor of any inheritance. We may not possess, use or dispose of anything without permission. Necessity gives us the right to ask but never the right to take...If we have ceased to consider ourselves as an individual we shall understand that we cannot deprive the Community of anything that would be to its advantage...As regards the fruits of our work all we earn is for the Community. We have no right to the profit of our labors.

I never thought that I would have to wrestle with the vow of poverty. A high school peer had asked me, "How can you leave all this?" I just shrugged. Material things didn't interest me that much. Even the appearance of riches embarrassed me like my dad's new Buick. But unlike nuns living in a monastery, poverty for semi-cloistered sisters had an element of relativity about it. Sisters were never to live better than the people they worked among. Had I been stationed in Africa or India I might have felt the pinch of poverty but not in Blue

Point. For the most part, our practice of poverty consisted in being detached from material things, in being frugal and circumspect in our use of things. We were to live in the spirit of poverty. Nonetheless, I did not expect to put my Holy Rule into practice as soon I did. During one visit in 1963 and after I took my first vows, my parents, who by now had the right to think I was settled, let me know they were writing their will and wanted to talk to me about it. My brother, who would soon graduate from Georgetown Law School, was also a part of this discussion. Did I want them to leave my half of their estate when they died to the Ursulines or not? Of course, my brother had a vested interest in the "or not." He promised to take care of me, if I should leave the convent, and I knew that he would. So all the scribbling in the copybook had a practical application after all. I had been a member of my family for seventeen years and a member of the Ursulines for three. My parents were people of modest means. The community was educating me which was something my parent's had not done. I am a Libra. Fair is fair. I told them that I thought my share should go to the Ursulines of Tildonk. Years later after I left the convent, and after my mother and father died, I saw the old will. My parents had left me their house.

I was soon to take a vow of obedience. I saw my little-girl self as pliant and ready to please. But that was only one part of my personality. I was generally obedient, but I always wanted to know the "why" of everything. However, "why" was not supposed to be in a sister's vocabulary. Everyone who knew me thought that obedience was going to be very difficult for me, and they were right. In my copybook I wrote:

> To learn the science of the religious life we must begin by learning to obey...A truly obedient religious is a miracle of grace. She submits both will and judgment which in God's eyes are worth more than fastings and many disciplines. We can never arrive at perfection without obedience...Strictly speaking there is only matter for sin when the Superior gives the order in the name of obedience. In the case of a formal order disobedience is a mortal sin. The

Church wishes that such commands be rare in order to insure that our wills are given freely to God and thus our religious habit may confer upon us the greatest dignity... It is true that from time to time obedience will demand heroic sacrifices...Let us love to obey blindly looking only to God.

I was never given a command that I flagrantly disobeyed. So I never committed a mortal sin of disobedience. The stakes were never that high, and I wasn't that important. But Martin Luther was given such a command, which he disobeyed and was punished by excommunication. In some quarters it's still debated whether that was such a good idea or not. The Jesuit, Teilhard de Chardin, a brilliant philosopher, paleontologist and geologist had his works censured and was ordered to sign a statement withdrawing his position about original sin. He obeyed. And I vaguely remember that Archbishop Fulton J. Sheen also had to make a crucial choice in favor of obedience. I believed the will of God was expressed through the will of the superior, but I struggled with blind obedience, and so I had lots of venial sins of disobedience to confess each week. But I think it would have been only a question of time, before I was faced with an order of greater magnitude.

The last vow to discuss is chastity -the vow that deals with sex and sexual pleasure. Our culture is supersaturated with sensual images and sounds via every possible media outlet. Sexual abstinence lies so far outside the normal experience, that years ago, one young woman in Spanish Harlem even asked my friend if she took a pill to stay chaste. With a smile and a chuckle, I can say, " no." But it is why I have spent a lot of time explaining how I was raised a Catholic, and a chaste young woman. I was not exposed to anything vulgar much less erotic. I associated with likeminded teenagers. I didn't smoke or drink nor did anyone in my group. I hadn't had a serious boyfriend or a passionate kiss. I didn't consider myself abnormal, because I knew others who were living the same way. I didn't even hear the word "masturbation" until I was in college. It was alluded to, of course. But I didn't do it. I was "saving myself." Finally, I wrote in my copybook about the vow of chastity:

Unlike poverty and obedience to wound the virtue is to sin against the vow. Chastity forms the matter of the vow because the state of virginity is more perfect than that of marriage. By the vow of chastity we understand A virginity and B chastity.

A we renounce marriage

B we bind ourselves by a vow to observe the sixth and ninth commandments...Let us avoid with particular care any unusual friendships...Do not desire to read everything that falls in your way...let us never touch others...The less we are in touch with people outside the safer we are.

The vow had to be better than its opposite. I could say to myself that it was better not to have sex than to have it. But then what I knew about sex was the same as what I knew about the Double Helix. Nothing. In prayer, I asked the Blessed Mary who DID have a baby, how not having a baby could be better than having one. Some of the most exquisite sculpture and paintings in the world portray the Madonna and child. I had very little experience with babies in my family since I was the youngest of two. My father was an only child and any extended family lived in Butler, Pennsylvania. I had never babysat for babies. I was willing to give up having a baby, mind you, but how could I say not having one was better than having one?

I thought myself sick. Somehow I'd stockpiled aspirins. Not easy considering all the permissions needed. I felt trapped. I even thought of jumping off the third story landing of the fire escape. Instead, I swallowed all the aspirins I had, and lay down on my bed, thinking I'd put an end to my pain. Very soon I was on my feet vomiting in the bathroom. All I had to do was walk down the stairs and out the door. Eventually, I would have found a phone, and my parents would have driven up to get me up as soon as they could. I had humiliated myself and no one knew about it. I had done much violence to my own psyche, and I had not shared it with my Novice Mistress. That, in itself, showed a great lack of humility. And the old binary, on/off thinking was still at work. Like many young women have done, (My mother told me her mother had serious doubts about her choice of mate but went ahead to avoid the embarrassment of calling off the wedding.) I went on with the "marriage" to Christ, even though I had serious reservations. It was God's will, wasn't it? We had listened to the radio when John Glenn became the first American in space on February 20th, 1962. While John Glenn and later Alan Shepard were flying into space, I was thinking of flying off the roof.

———

I was emotionally depleted and depressed. March was dreary and drizzly one day and nice another. I wrote home:

> *We had a nice surprise last night and I was just in the mood for it. A motion picture full length on the Trapp family...A good movie is a real treat. Today is beautiful. Glenn will be glad. Will you see it on T.V. the parade I mean...*

> *Dear Mom I wish you would sit down and write more often. I love to hear from you and it would be just like a little pen chat. It would do us both good. Mother Genevieve hardly reads family mail (they just don't have time) but she told me explicitly she wouldn't read your letters. So I'll be the only one to see them and I'll rip them right up when I'm finished. Keep me in your prayers and you know you're always in mine. Take it easy. God love you. Your loving daughter, Sister Mary Christine*

That was very considerate of my Novice Mistress and my mother did write back to me and sent a duet book for piano, but her letters were still rare. Three weeks later on March 25, 1962 I wrote to her:

Dear Mom,

So glad to hear from you. I hope you are feeling better. I think the change of the seasons pulls everybody down a little bit too. The weather is so beautiful. We just came back from our Sunday walk down to the Bay. It makes you feel glad to be alive.

...Yesterday was Sr. Gabrielle's feast day and we put on a show for her. It was more like an amateur hour. Anyway Sr. Domenica and I played "La Cinqtain." (sic) It's Spanish I think and Sr. Gabrielle gives Spanish lessons. So it was quite appropriate. Sr. Aloysius and Sr. Amadeus played "Shortn'Bread". We had fun. They weren't perfect but it was pretty good for two days practice (about 10 minutes each sitting)... But Sr. Gabrielle enjoyed it and so did we....

...Can't wait to see you. But the best news of all is about Dad. I'm simply thrilled. You didn't give me much information though. Will it be at Red Bank or near-by? Does he have to have a sponsor and a name?...well, we certainly have a lot to thank God for.

My father was going to be confirmed in the Catholic Church. At long last he would become a real Catholic. I felt God had answered my prayers and that this transformation of my father was directly due to the fact, that I took myself to the more difficult life in the semi-cloistered Ursulines, rather than to the community that had educated me in New Jersey. It wasn't Father Neuman's doing after all. He'd only pointed the way. I had deliberately chosen the steeper mountain. I had made a bargain with God and I told no one. He had delivered, so I'd better too. I also had another pact realized. Ursulines were expected to sit upright in chairs and in pews for the rest of their lives if they weren't sick. This, I thought, was a difficult mortification, so I offered it to God for my Uncle Marvin. He was a sensitive soul who was an alcoholic long before it was considered a disease. And God took care of him too. Marvin stopped drinking twelve years before he died. He took loving care of both his father and mother until their deaths. So essentially I was still lighting candles to get a bike. But the candles now were my life and the bike was souls. I would make my vows come June. I had not yet learned about magical thinking.

We were in the midst of a sea change, as my father would say. The Second Vatican Ecumenical Council was opened under Pope John XXIII in 1962. My father, like a lot of other Christians, really liked John XXIII. The Pope not only opened windows. He opened doors. And my father, a poor excuse for a Catholic and a lame excuse for a Lutheran, let the fresh air invigorate him and that's really why my father decided to be confirmed in the Catholic Church. Change was in the air. You could taste it and smell it like ozone. It was electrifying and terrifying at the same time. Directives were coming from our motherhouse in Belgium. I wrote to my parents in April, 1962:

> *Don't throw away your Latin books! … If people were hoping for an English Mass to emerge from the coming Council they better change their hopes. It's hard to believe the Council will start in five months. …Please pray for me too. Beg God to give me the graces I need to prepare for Holy Profession just about 85 days away now. I am so very happy Dad, and even when I'm not happy, I am always at peace. God takes but He gives too.*

Admitting to my father that I was not always happy is a significant departure from earlier letters. Clearly I did not have a crystal ball. One change that is hardly worth mentioning had to do with how we held our hands in the refectory during grace before meals. Previously, we held our hands palm to palm with fingers pointing heavenward and thumbs crossed. Shakespeare's Juliet said it so much better. "For saints have hands that pilgrim's hands do touch. And palm to palm is holy palmers' kiss" 1.5.100. Now we were told that we would not hold our hands thusly; but would interlace our fingers in a clutch position. I remember such minutiae because I still wasn't free to choose which way to hold my hands. It drove me crazy. With progress like this I despaired of ever seeing more important, substantive changes in religious life. I was having a hard time stifling the "whys."

I was teaching Confraternity of Christian Doctrine classes On Wednesdays I had a class of young unruly boys. I wrote home:

> *At least about 75% of the boys were very good this week especially for about the first 30 minutes. ... Well only a short time til Profession. Tomorrow we start the 6 wks preparation. We have extra meditations on the Vows and Religious life etc. At the end of the 6 wks, we have an 8 day retreat...No matter How much we have to give, God will not be outdone in generosity. But I don't think He minds a few tears because He understands. I was so happy to hear about Marvin. I would love them to be at my Profession very much. Be seeing you in two weeks.*

This was a very busy time. The novices and postulants were spring-cleaning for Easter. Scrubbing the tiles in the parlor bathroom in straight ammonia gave me blinding, pounding sick headaches, so I asked permission and was allowed to go to bed. Painters were in the convent painting the sewing room in pink and the floor in white. We laughed to hear men whistling in the convent. There were more changes in the habit.

> *I lost 45 minutes of a precious Sunday afternoon – we tried on the new bonnets – they don't have any band under the neck – maybe we'll have them on for Easter.*

At the end of May I wrote:

> *Our new robes are finished. We get new everything for Profession, bandeaux, dickies, shoes – the works. Every now and again Mother Vicar takes us for a practice for the Ceremony and that counts for one of the extra meditations. We practiced the hymns this afternoon. The*

six of us have some parts to chant alone. Bye now. God
love you. Your loving daughter. Sister Mary Christine

A month before profession, the good Father made an unexpected visit to Blue Point and asked to see me. Visits were especially important to me because they were so rare. The rest of my group had entered under the wing of a teaching sister. She was called their *gumba* from the Italian slang for friend or pal and they might see her from time to time at Blue Point. They always knew they had someone rooting for them, someone in their corner, someone asking about their progress. I entered not knowing anyone and this probably contributed to my intense feeling of loneliness. So I hurried to the parlor with happy expectancy. I really wanted to talk to him about my feelings and doubts. I tentatively began to speak about the upcoming profession with a question in my voice, but he changed the subject. He gave me exactly thirty-five minutes. I was scheduled to play the organ for the 8th grade graduation in the Lady of the Snow Church at Blue Point. When he left, I raced upstairs changed into my black veil and ran down to the Church. I had missed the march but was there for the rest.

On June 26, 1962, six second year novices processed into the Chapel once again. We had lost another one. Our white veils were deftly removed and black veils were positioned on our heads. We each made our temporary profession of vows of poverty, chastity and obedience for three years to Reverend Mother Vicar in front of the community and guests. My parents, brother, Grandmother Kerr and Uncle Marvin all came to Blue Point to celebrate with me. The Father also came. My parents gave me a watch for a gift and a croquet set and a set of fins to use swimming. Gifts were handed in to the superior and she disposed of them as she saw fit. The watch was given to me to use. The sisters made a fuss over my beloved Grandmother Roxy and she enjoyed the attention.

First Profession June 26, 1962
Uncle Marvin, Mom, Sr. Christine, Grandma Roxy Kerr, Bill

One of the novices knew shorthand and took down the sermon that was delivered at our profession. I sent a copy home.

...If your sisters in the world who were married yesterday, or getting married today or tomorrow are just beginning a tremendous task that they will have to work, suffer all their lives to make the dream come true or else they make a mess of their lives. You who are marrying Christ like them are just beginning. You will have to work and suffer just like the human marriage with all

the human weaknesses of the world. And as a mother of a family in the world has once again to spend her last breath to make her dream come true the same holds true for these young women...

I was twenty.

**Sr. Christine and Father Neumann
First Profession 1962**

⟞⟋⟍⟍⟋⟋⟞

Now that we had professed our vows for three years and wore black veils, we were called Junior professed or Juniors. We no longer belonged in the novitiate. The large second floor room with a glassed in porch looking out to the bay had been a safe harbor for three years. I had a Novice Mistress who knew my soul better than I did. I had cried there and suffered and laughed there and had lots of fun there. I grew up in that room. But it was time to move on.

The six of us packed up our things and moved into a small cape on the grounds. It was called the Annex and it required some adjusting on our part. In the novitiate our cubicles were small but at least they were our own. Now we were two to a bedroom. When I returned to it, I found that my roommate would have straightened my shoes just so. I certainly knew about obsessive behavior, but I still didn't like it. We were not compatible. The bathroom facilities in the novitiate were more than adequate, but now in this cape there were seven women sharing one bathroom. It could be a long wait in the evening. If you deferred to your sisters there might not be enough hot water. We had a living room with a T.V. We had just a few chores assigned because our main job was to go to school full time. We had Chapter now only once a week instead of every day. We assembled in the library with the older sisters. We went first and then left. Our immediate superior, Mother Berchmans, was nice enough, but she wasn't that involved and didn't get to know us very well. We went to her for our ordinary permissions. It seemed quite perfunctory in light of the intensive attention we had received in the novitiate. However, Mother Ursula continued to take an interest in us and our studies. I remember standing in the parlor reciting a memorized French poem by Paul Verlaine while she listened attentively. Anything needed for school she provided. Books assigned by professors were never scrutinized. My brother expressed surprise that I had read a novel by Graham Greene probably *The Power and the Glory*. The new sense of freedom was exhilarating; even though, we still had Sr. Kevin, a professed sister, living at the house to keep an eye on us. We had barely settled in before we were sent to Our Lady of Grace convent in Howard Beach for the summer.

I had signed up to take two courses at St. John's University in Jamaica. This time we would be on campus in real classrooms with regular students. No more "home schooling." Howard Beach was an easy commute to the university. I could see Idlewild (now JFK) from the roof of the convent, which was so tall it was equipped with a flashing light to warn pilots. I could just about wave to them as they passed overhead. There is much enthusiasm in my letter home:

I think I told you we're taking physics and History of Education. Each day of summer school is worth about a week so they really keep you going. Sr. Angelus and I went to Sr. John's on Friday with Sr. Joseph (Mr. Lynch drove) to check for Sept. As it stands we will be able to master in both English and Psychology. We went in the Cadillac. I think it's the lst time I've ever been in one. Sr. Angelus and I had the whole back seat going in. What fun. Every window goes up and down by buttons.

The community had acquired the caddy in the previous year through a lottery the Bishop held. The three communities that had motherhouses in his diocese- Dominican, St. Joseph and Ursulines - got to put their names in. The Ursulines won.

At the beginning of the summer I had asked Mother Vicar if I could start to drive the community car back and forth to Bayport and the beach. And she said, yes. I got my license in high school. I can thank my brother for that because every time I asked my dad to take me out driving he showed me how to change a tire. I didn't have a great driving record, though. I remember in senior year making a tight right turn onto Spring St. and wrapping my father's new blue and white Buick around a telephone pole. My dad made me go to the dealer to get it fixed. Thankfully, my best friend, Joan, came with me. She felt bad because she had insisted I drive her home when I wanted her to stay over. A woman walked around the dented car going "Tsk, tsk, tsk, did you do that?" I said "yes." The Vice Principal, Sr. Teresina, gave us both detentions because we were late getting into homeroom. I didn't tell Reverend Mother that story.

I wrote home July 2, 1962:

It's July 3 and I'm sitting down at Bayport. You'll never guess what I did. I made three round trips from

87

*the house to the Bay – driving the car. I thought I
would be too afraid. But I wasn't, the station wagon
drives very smoothly.*

Staying at Our Lady of Grace convent in Howard Beach was my
first taste of what it would be like to live out in the houses. At this
time, the community's sole mission was elementary education. We
got up to say the Office, meditate and hear Mass. Breakfast was
usually in silence. Then we were in the car and off to St. John's. I
found it stimulating. I loved school, and I loved studying. When I
first wrote to Mother Vicar as a high school graduate, I told her that
I would like to study science. Of course by now, I knew that a good
nun would study what she was told to study. But I got an A+ in Inte-
grated Physical Science all the same, and just an A in the History of
Education. Our Superior, Mother Benignus, was kind and indulgent.
We could sit out in the patio in the evening and watch the airplanes
fly overhead. There were magnificent sunsets, probably because of
the pollution hanging over New York City. We would make up stories about the planes and pilots flying overhead and be silly. There
was also a small room with a grand piano in it and, more important,
there was enough free time to use it. When I was five, my Grandmother Kerr taught me how to play the piano. After we moved to
New Jersey, my mom oversaw my playing. There were other sisters
far more musically talented than I was. But I did what I was told and
played the organ when needed and also led children's choirs. There
is a definite advantage in doing God's will as expressed by the superior. Whatever happens, it's to the good. If you mess up, then you
offer that to God in humility. If you succeed, then it's God's will, so
you can't be puffed up about it. Either way, it's a win-win. For me, a
timid and immature person, that approach to life was like attaching
training-wheels to a bike. It took away the fear of falling and failing.

——⟋∕∕⟍——

I was sent to the convent at Howard Beach for the summer
because it was a close commute to St. John's University where I was
taking History, English and Adolescent Psychology.

88

In July I wrote:

Finals were Friday and boy am I bushed. We left Howard Beach Friday afternoon for Blue Point. I'm out in the garden writing this now. We're sleeping down at Bayport. It's beautiful at night, you can hear the waves lapping against the beach – delicious...we go swimming in the afternoon and can go in at night too, if we want before we go to bed...It has been a hot summer...I got a letter from Grandma B. She seems all right now and in good spirits.

My dad's mom, Grandma B, was now eighty-six years old. She had been writing letters addressed to Sr. Louis Marie, my look alike. I'm not sure how she got confused. I suggested to my parents that they put address labels on envelopes. My parents came out to visit me at Blue Point in July. I wrote home in September, 1962:

The sisters are all back from Ireland. They all gained weight and freckles too. Sr. Joseph has to start reducing on account of her heart. There were three bishops on the boat with her and Ralph Bunche from the U.N. She was talking to all of them of course. She is quite the person that way.

These Irish sisters had not been home since they entered the convent as teenagers more than forty years before. Many of their parents were deceased. A few even had siblings born after they had left home. It had to have been an emotional visit. In hindsight, I think they would also have been dropped into the middle of the continuing violent struggle between Ireland and Great Britain. By 1962 it was clear the Irish Republican Army's latest campaign against Northern Ireland had failed. It would be nearly impossible for the political unrest of their homeland not to influence the Irish sisters' personal feelings toward their English born Mother Vicar. I continued in the same letter:

I can't wait to show you my textbooks. We're been back at school for a week now and almost in routine... you would laugh to see us start out in the morning... Our thermoses and lunches are packed in red plaid bags. Each of us has a little picnic set in our locker at St. John's in the "nun's room." A lounge just for us nuns, ha! ...We register to vote on October 6. I'll be old enough to vote in November.

The "nun's lounge" kept us from unnecessary mingling with college students in the cafeteria. Teaching practices at that time did not promote group work, and that was fine with me because I had never liked the few group projects assigned in high school. I didn't like the idea that my grade would depend on other people's efforts. But it meant that I never interacted with the college students at all. Nor did I belong to any clubs or societies. Our long commute from Blue Point precluded such involvement. Only later when writing resumes did I understand what I had missed.

In this long letter home I mention that Gladys and Gordon, two friends from high school, dropped in unexpectedly for a visit and I was able to sit with them from 5:30 to 6:00 when the bell rang for supper. ... *I did most of the talking and I would gather that about 95% of the motivation to see me was curiosity, ha! How I love the aloofness of Blue Point...* Well of course they were curious about an old friend who had effectively dropped off the radar screen.

At last I was old enough to vote. Mother Ursula had a little smile on her face when she sent us off to the polls suggesting we vote for certain local candidates. She knew that we knew she couldn't tell us how to vote. We were, after all, Americans and not Belgian boarding school girls. Her humor was subtle. I don't think I ever heard her give a hearty laugh or saw her with a broad smile on her face, but then she was the Mother Superior.

My week was full. On Mondays I sat in classes from 10:00 to 6:00. Tuesdays I was home. Wednesdays I had two classes which finished at 3:50. Thursday I had to make the drive in for one class from 2:00 to 4:00 and on Fridays the day went from 10:00 to 4:00. We had two cars and took turns driving. They had no radios, so we'd pray the rosary and then study or talk. Every day held the unexpected. Once we had a blowout on the Sunrise Highway going at least 65 miles per hour. The station wagon with eight sisters and all their heavy book bags swerved wildly into the median strip until eventually we came to a stop. There were deep skid marks in the soft grass. For a few wild seconds, I thought my end had come. We were promptly rescued, and a kind man changed our tire, and off we went to St. John's. I was so glad I was not driving that day. Had the accident happened when we were closer to the city, where there was no median strip, we would have suffered fatalities. Once I was sitting in the backseat indulging in a full unladylike yawn, when a man passed us and shook his finger at me. During another evening ride home, we passed a rattle trap car with no lights. One passenger, a tough looking young lad, rapidly blessed himself when he saw all the nuns in the car. I guess he thought we were bad luck. Another winter night after driving endless hours through a blinding snowstorm, we got home very late. We walked in like bedraggled dolls, and went straight to the Chapel, because it was time for Vespers. What I really felt we needed was a group hug and hot chocolate.

On October 18, 1962 I turned 21. My letters throughout the winter were full of school news and the continuing ill health of Pope John XXIII. My parents were able to travel to Washington, D.C. on June 9th and 10th for my brother's graduation from Georgetown Law School. He invited me, of course, but I could not go. My parent's visits to Blue Point had to accommodate their schedule and mine. I wrote to my dad sometime in June, 1963:

> *I'm sure you and Mom enjoyed yourselves down at DC. I can't wait to hear about it. Sat. is a good day to come and I'll be expecting you. I bet you'll be tired. Bill won't be home in time to come out will he? I think Mom said he had another week of proctoring to do.*
>
> *We followed the Pope's agony and death through the retreat. He is certainly a real inspiration to everyone... We went to the Solemn High Requiem Mass on Mon at St. Agnes Cathedral in Rockville Center. I had never seen a High Mass said by a Bishop. It is very beautiful.*

A funny thing happened the other day. Every 5 yrs the Bishop has to send a report to Rome concerning all under his care, business, finance, spiritual matters etc. Well he sends a delegate to each convent to see all the sisters one by one. It's a safeguard. Well, anyway, Sister Domenica is Italian and she gets a real tan. She has been sitting out in the sun lately. The poor Msgr. has poor eyesight to top it off. His eyes were half closed. Anyway Sr. D goes in. He asks her name and she tells him. " Is that a Spanish name," he asked. "No," she said. That was her 1ˢᵗ clue. Later on he asked her if she had any integration problems like down in Alabama ha! She went along with him (how could you get out of it) and said "Oh, no all of us are Americans." I still laugh every time I see her.

Well, Dad I'll save anymore news for Sat. By then I should know where I'll be for the summer. Can't wait to see you... Your loving daughter, Sister Mary Christine, RU PS xx (We're listening to JFK record!! Vol 1 very funny)

This is what I wrote home, but I remember also going in for the interview with the Monsignor and being asked if I thought the Italian sisters were treated differently from the rest of the sisters. For that question to even arise, someone must have felt they were being treated unfairly and in some way the message was forwarded to the Bishop. I believe "dropped a dime" is the common expression. I told the Monsignor I hadn't seen it. Of course I was only one year out of the novitiate and living as a Junior sister at Blue Point, what did I know.

In my post script I mention that we listened to a JFK record and found it humorous. Someone had brought us *The First Family* record by Vaughn Meader - perhaps my folks. We didn't think it was disrespectful laughing at a parody of Jacqueline's whispery boarding school voice and Jack's Boston Brahmin vowels and nonexistent "r-endings". It was a ribbing we might dish out to our own family members. We all thought it really funny and clever. But it was a cruel joke because in only five months President Kennedy would be assassinated, and that record would never be played again.

On October 1, 1963 I wrote home informing my parents of the next visiting day. I told them about meeting Father Bishoff at St. John's. I literally screamed out his name and started running toward him just like in the movies. Then when I caught up with him I didn't know whether to kiss him or shake hands. I did shake his hand and then couldn't think of a thing to say. He was at the school to see about finishing his thesis for a doctorate. He had taught the marriage course at my high school and was well liked by all. I had been away from home for so long that seeing someone from my former life in New Jersey was like a vision. Another time I was going into a building at St. John's and a boy said, "Buenos dias." I had a dumb look on my face until I realized that Sister Louis Marie, my look-a-like, had taken Spanish in the summer. He caught on and told me to tell her "Hola." I replied we look alike but aren't really sisters and he said, "Well, you are sisters in religion."

My dad's fifty-sixth birthday was November 8th. I sent him a card with a note.

> *Remember Eddie Mayoff in That's My Boy well my Personality Psych teacher is just like him, looks and all except he's thinner. I wish you could come to some of my classes – you would get a kick out of it. If you see Bill tell him if he'd come a week later I would have known all about Edith Piaf and Jacques Cos- teau. Our French teacher told us about them and we had a couple of lectures on them. The French club showed La Belle et La Bete which I saw and enjoyed. It was by Cocteau and in French. One of the sisters received a record called Soeur Sourire. It is songs written and sung by a Domenican nun of Belgium. She plays a Spanish guitar and sings the alto to her own voice – records them together. You should tell my brother to get a hold of it...*

We really liked the music of *Soeur Sourire*. She was "Sister Smile" in French but the "Singing Nun" to us. So we learned the songs in English and French. They were peppy and easy to memorize. *Dominique, nique, nique* was our favorite. I found out later that *Soeur Sourire* was the only Belgian artist who wrote and sang her way to number one on the American charts. This young woman became a celebrity while a religious. However, the essence of being a religious is antithetical to the essence of being a celebrity. At 33 she left the community. Phillips, the company who made her first record, owned the name, *Soeur Sourire* so she could no longer use it. Most of the profits were split between Phillips and the Dominican order but the government hounded her for back taxes. Her efforts to regain success were futile. Sadly on March 29, 1985 at age 51 Jeanne Dekkers and her partner committed suicide. Now she lives on UTube.

⟬⟭⟬⟭

A new Catholic Archdiocesan High School was to be built in Huntington, Long Island and staffed by three different religious communities. Mother Ursula wanted to be ready to supply teachers for this school, because up until then the Ursulines staffed only parish grammar schools. Sisters would now need to hold Master degrees. I was told I would be majoring in English and minoring in psychology for a BA degree to be followed by a Masters in a field to be yet decided.

As there were many forces leading me to adopt religious life, so there were equally as many factors leading me to renounce my vows, but the study of psychology was foremost. It opened up new ways for me to look at myself and look at the decision I had made to become a nun.

I was glad I hadn't chosen the field of psychology voluntarily, because I found the professors unusual and different in speech and behavior. I can only imagine what they thought of me – a young woman sitting in black with her hands folded on the edge of the desk. But as always, I studied diligently, did my papers and got all A's except in Statistics. Innocently I didn't know I would soon become a statistic myself. These psych professors were constantly writing papers and needing subjects to study. I took the Myers-Briggs Personality Test for the first time. The psych department asked for willing volunteers for projects and I offered to participate in other, now forgotten, psychological experiments.

Of course, I had as many personal issues to explore as do all students of psychology. My mother's distance was one of them. Her obsessive-compulsive behavior was another. I learned about my automatic reactions to difficulties called *defense mechanisms*. I now understood that our vigorous training in the novitiate was intended to break those down. For example, stop blaming someone else, or the weather, or the baker, if the bread couldn't be cut straight. Take responsibility. I learned that free will and self-determination could be mitigated by many things. I learned about the hierarchy of our basic human needs according to Maslow. For the first time I studied sex. And I learned the term *sublimation*. I started to look at the male teachers differently. I had thoughts unbecoming a nun if not downright impure which I confessed to a priest I believed wasn't fluent in English. I started to see myself as a sexual being with needs and wants. And more important, I learned that those needs and wants were normal. I learned the word *repression*. This was a Catholic university run by the Vincentian Fathers and no professor who wanted to keep his or her job was going to say celibacy was abnormal. But slowly, slowly, I began to question who I was, and what I was doing in the convent. The convent ironically provided me with the luxury of three years of unlimited time to study and read. Only in my 50s, and then only for one year, did I enjoy such a pure indulgence again. Our psych tests were always multiple choice and graded on the devilish bell curve. Sometimes, I ruined it for my fellow students by doing well, and they weren't happy. But how many students had an entire day to study for one test?

In Child Psychology I learned about Maria Montessori and realized that my Grandmother Bassler had provided my brother and me with the best preschool environment anyone could have wished for. I wrote to her and told her just that. On rainy days she'd empty the blanket chest that had once carried great-grandfather Gottlieb's belongings across the sea, and it became a magical ship; on sunny days she'd throw a blanket over a clothesline and we'd set up an African camp. Our blocks were discarded thread spools from her beautiful braided rugs. We picked blackberries on the hills during the day, and played cards at night and made fudge on a whim letting it cool on the windowsill. We went to sleep hearing wonderful stories about dogs that managed to travel miles getting home on their own. My brother and I started school in first grade. Nursery school didn't exist where we lived, and my mother couldn't afford kindergarten, but thanks to Grandma B, it didn't hold us back in the least.

Studying psychology insinuated the idea that my striving for perfection and my desire for sainthood were merely compensatory thinking for a garden variety, inferiority complex. I was discovering myself as a person and as a woman. Maybe I wasn't on a holy enterprise after all. It gave rise to the thought that perhaps my pursuit of God was just a habit.

Serving mom in the guest dining room June, 1963

November 22, 1963 our Catholic President John Fitzgerald Kennedy was shot. Everyone knows where they were when they heard the news and so do I. I was doing research in the temporary library in a basement at St. John's. When we headed back to

Blue Point later that afternoon, we said the rosary for his recovery. Without a radio in the car we knew nothing more. The grief everyone felt at the news of his death overwhelmed us. We sat riveted in front of the T.V. in the Annex and watched with the rest of America as he was put to rest and we cried. I remember sitting on the lower step of the staircase in the Annex sobbing. I couldn't stop the tears. I was crying for him, for our country and for me. I had a feeling that the others watching me sensed, as I did, that my copious tears had broken through some kind of long pent up emotional dam. My mom's birthday was December 22nd and I sent her a card.

> *Happy Birthday! I played hooky from school today. Just couldn't wait for the vacation to start. Classes stop at twelve today and then the students have a Christmas party. I couldn't bear the trip in and out for just one class, so Rev. Mother let Sr. Aloysius and me play hooky. The novices are busy cleaning. I read somewhere that if you get your World's Fair tickets before Jan. 1964 you can get a 10% discount and you can buy as many as you want...When you buy the shoes would you please get soft rubber heels put on. The shoes come with rubber heels but they are hard rubber and I have to get them changed because they make too much noise in the monastery ha! Thanks a lot. I know you'll have a Happy Birthday. I will remember you very specially in my Mass and Communion on the 23rd. Be seeing you soon. Love your daughter.*

My mom was now fifty-five. Besides the obsessive-compulsive behavior mentioned earlier, she also suffered from depression exacerbated by menopause. I felt helpless to comfort her and felt guilty about not being at home to help. A month earlier I had written to my father:

> *Mama seemed better last visit but it is hard to tell whether that was just a good day or an improvement. Please God it will let up in time. You have had to bear*

97

the brunt of it, the daily grind. I'm sorry I haven't been able to help more. It has been quite a cross for both Mama and you. It is so heartbreaking because it seems like such a useless silly waste. Excuse the preaching. But God knows best... yesterday was our retreat day, ha! And I'm all shined up for the week...

I hoped my words offered my father some comfort but these stock phrases were all I had at my disposal. My parents did get tickets to the New York World's Fair, and they went often. I eventually went in the summer. Maybe I could have met them there for an afternoon, but I didn't ask permission. These were the kind of small daily mortifications and exercises in detachment that I offered up to God, but perhaps I didn't have the humility to ask for the necessary permissions.

I wrote home in 1964 about the celebration of our Mother Superior's fifty years in the convent:

We celebrated Mother Vicar's Jubilee on Thursday. What a wonderful day it was. All of the sisters came down. We sung the High Mass. The Chapel is really beautiful. There are new gold curtains hanging behind the altar. The whole house is decorated in gold. After Mass, Mother Vicar opened some presents in the parlor and the photographer came to take our picture outside the house. After that we all went to Felice's for a catered dinner. What a lovely room we were in. We really had a wonderful time. You can imagine no dishes and work etc. the community sisters got up and sang during courses. When we came home about 4:00 we, Juniors, put on a show followed by the novices' Pinafore which was really excellent. Then we went up to the novitiate which we had set up earlier for a buffet supper. Quite a day. The actual day of the M.Vicar's Jubilee is on the 25th so we're going to celebrate that too.

—cৎৎৎ—

I was sent to the Nativity of the Blessed Virgin in Ozone Park for the next summer session. I was taking Shakespeare, Secondary School Methods, English and Marriage and the Family with a wonderful priest, Fr. Hansberger. My parents must have wondered what I was doing taking a course on Marriage. It was a theology course so the emphasis was on relationships. I liked it. Or I liked Fr. Hansberger. I also loved Shakespeare. I wrote home in June:

> *The other night after Shakespeare class (goes from 6:20-7:35 P.M.) an elderly lady approached me and said she was of the Jewish faith and could I help her. She wanted to know what prayer we said before class even though everybody was saying it she couldn't understand it (which doesn't say much for us) Anyhow, I wrote the Hail Mary out for her and she was grateful. She said her brother years before had won a scholarship to St. John's Law school and now she was going. There are a lot of quite old people going and I often wonder about the circumstances.*

Ah youth, my parents must have been thinking. I was twenty-three, so even if they were only forty or fifty, I would have thought them ancient.

My mother and Grandmother Kerr had gone to the 1939 New York World's Fair by train from Butler, Pennsylvania. It too was held at Flushing Meadows. Revisiting the fairgrounds twenty-five years later must have been a bitter-sweet experience for my mother. This time she went often with her husband and on one occasion brought her mother-in-law, Grandma B. Businessmen in 1939 thought the U.S. society coming out of the Great Depression needed a shot in the arm, and in 1964 they thought society needed a great distraction from the Vietnam War. Shots in the arm always get my attention.

Sister Christine and Grandma B, age 87 in September 1964

I wrote a long letter describing my visit to the World's Fair. I had a good time. I knew my father would be pleased I went to the American Society of Electrical Engineers that had a demonstration complete with lights, music and water. I saw the Sweden, Malaysia, Sudan and Jordan pavilions. Jordan let us in free. Downstairs they were showing a film on Holy Week in Jerusalem. Japan displayed appliances and little TVs. Mexico had guitar music. I especially liked the American Pavilion that showed a movie about the development of America, emphasizing the melting pot idea and then offered a car ride through a tunnel of screens showing the history of US. But even though the Fair was a great distraction I wrote: *I'll be glad when the summer is over – only about four more weeks. Looking forward to seeing you in September.*

The truth was I didn't feel as comfortable at this convent any-more. There were quite a few younger Professed who were also going to summer school. They hadn't had the opportunity to go to college full time as my group was doing. I felt they held some resentment about that. Many sisters had taken the same courses at St. John's so that there was a great collection of term papers passed around like a box of tissues. " You have a paper due, when? Here have one." I naturally was shocked as only the self-righteous can be. I was very hard on myself, and so I was very hard on everybody else. Real saints wouldn't be like that. I never SAID anything to them or anybody else, but nuns have a sixth sense for a lot of things. So I'm sure they were glad to see me return to Blue Point.

On September 8, 1964 I wrote:

> *I'm only going in to St. John's two days a week on Tuesday and Thursday so it will be a pretty easy year. I think of you sailing away on the Sursum Corda when I'm lying on the beach. There are some beauti-ful sailboats on the Bay.*

> *Today is entrance day. Just think five years ago to-day we drove out. Remember we were early and had dinner together in the dining room. Boy! How time flies. Four of the six sisters in my group left Sunday for their teaching assignments...*

Most of my group moved to their new teaching assignments. I was left behind because I was carrying a double major. So I had one more year to go. The fall semester was easy: Readings in European Literature, the Modern Novel, and a Survey of Historical Scholas-tic Philosophy. We usually drove home from St. John's in time for Vespers. After supper in the refectory, we'd return to the Annex where we watched the evening news. Every night the Vietnam body counts were displayed. I wondered how there could be any more enemy soldiers left to fight if the numbers were true. I became disillusioned with the government. Once when I walked around the back of a building at St. John's, I saw a small demonstration of students holding placards protesting the war. That evening on the news the camera angle made it look like hundreds were demonstrating. I became equally disillusioned with the media. My views were not shared by most and I stopped watching the evening news.

I was also doing Practice Teaching at our school, St. William the Abbot in Seaford. This was a lovely school and convent in an upscale neighborhood. I liked it, but I also didn't feel comfortable. I didn't understand how each convent was governed in the context of the whole community. It didn't seem right to me that sisters living in a more affluent parish might have more comfortable surroundings than sisters living in a poorer parish. I didn't really have anyone to talk to about these issues.

———⟨ΘΛΘ⟩———

My dad had another birthday. In November 1964 I wrote:

I'm filling out a form to apply for a National Science Foundation grant in Psychology. There's only a 1-4 chance of winning one but it's worth it to try. You get $2,400 and tuition and courses paid for. My grades are good and I can get recommendations. In December I take the aptitude test. This is just a general test of your verbal and math skills. In January the psychology test is given. So keep me in your prayers – you never know. I'm applying for an assistantship too. St. John's foots the bill but I would have to put in about 12 hours a week.

In either case I'll be going for a MA in Experimental Psych. Here's a list of the courses involved: Perception, History of Psych, Advanced Psych, Laboratory Statistics, Experimental Design, Physiological Psych, Brain...Pretty good ha! Dear Dad what can I give you for your birthday- nothing but my love and my prayers. If it is so painful to grow up and live sepa-

rated from you and Mama it is only because of the
love, closeness and happiness of our home and my
childhood. To love more means to suffer more. I
wouldn't change anything; it is worth it.

Clearly my education is important to me and a multitude of opportunities was being offered which in retrospect looks like they weren't sure where or how to use me. I thought my dad would want to know that I was being challenged academically. I was excited about all the possible future avenues of study. A 1964 December birthday card to my mother continues with more pious platitudes and bromides. I meant them sincerely but I also knew they were of no practical help whatsoever. I felt impotent.

I'm grateful to God for giving me such a good and
loveable mother (and the best cook in the world)
God will see us through all our sufferings and will
sanctify us in His love in His own way – you at home
and me here in the convent.

P.S. Please pray for our sisters in the Congo. Some
of the sisters of other communities who were killed
came from around Ozone Park and our sisters knew
them. We feel very saddened by what has happened...

The situation in the Republic of the Congo became life threatening. Over eight hundred Belgians and sixty Americans had been taken hostage in Stanleyville. Belgium and the United States began secret plans for the U.S. Air force to provide the aircraft, deliver troops and support to the hostages. The rescued would be airlifted to Leopoldville and then to Europe. It took about two days to rescue almost 2,000 hostages. Unfortunately, twenty-eight hostages had been gunned down in the square in front of the Victoria Hotel, and two Belgian soldiers were killed and eleven wounded. We prayed for peace.

I had a heavy school schedule in the spring: Statistical Methods for Social Science, European Literature, Survey History of Scholas-tic Philosophy and the Short Story. In February 1965, I sent my parents a letter on pink paper cut in the shape of a heart. I reassured my mother that I was practicing the piano and had started learning the 12th *Street Rag*. I also put together a *Hymn to St. Angela*. I took a theme line from Handel's Largo, made up a line of my own, repeated it then repeated Handel's and I had a new hymn. I put the words to the Collect of her Mass to the music. I'm not sure it was ever sung. We were now rising at 8:15 instead of 6:00.

Because our letters were no longer being opened, my mother started to write to me. In March 1965, I wrote back:

> *Thanks for the nice letter last week, Mom. I was glad to hear of the nice week the Keck's had. Tomorrow I go in to Seaford to teach geography. The lesson is on California. Eighth graders keep you on your toes, ha! Last week Madame Von Trapp spoke at Seaton Hall High School which is in Patchogue. Mother Vicar and the sisters who were at home that day went over to hear her. They were very much impressed...*

My parents had visited the Trapp Family Lodge in Vermont. They even got Maria's autograph on a postcard, which I still have. Dad also got interested in the recorder and bought one for me as well. He had played the trumpet in high school so the recorder was a good deal easier. My parents came out to visit me faithfully. The April visit was a real sacrifice for my mother because my Grandmother Kerr had died April 26th. They visited me on Saturday and were returning with my brother to Pennsylvania on Sunday for the wake and funeral. If either my parents or I had asked Mother Vicar, I think she would have permitted me to accompany them. But they didn't and I didn't. I'd like to think it was virtue on my part. But once again I seemed to lack the humility to expose my feelings and the level of attachment I still had for my family by seeking special exceptions. I wrote home:

> *...Thank God she didn't have to linger longer than she did. But even though we knew the end was near, the*

grief at her loss is still very painful. How few people have the close relationship to their grandparents as I have had with mine? I appreciate this friendship and am grateful for Grandma's influence upon me. I thank you very sincerely for making this possible. Grandma could not have died in a more beautiful season. The hope of the resurrection permeates every prayer and how much more it is our hope too.

My Grandma Kerr was a special person. She was a solid, hardworking, no nonsense woman. She voted for Adlai Stevenson because he was family through the Fell's on her paternal grandmother's side. Sensibly religious, she went to Mass every Sunday and demanded all who slept under her roof to do the same. Unfortunately, her marriage wasn't made in heaven, and her youngest son was the cause of much worry for most of her life. Grandpa worked on the B&O railroad from the time he was sixteen until he was seventy. He always brought his paycheck home, and didn't drink, but he had a quick, volatile temper. During the five years we lived with them my brother and I often heard loud angry words and slamming doors, but our Grandfather never raised his voice to us. Grandma remained devoted to her family. Besides teaching me how to play the piano, she taught me how to crochet and knit. I watched her quilt, and I watched her bake. We played endless Canasta games. After moving to New Jersey we visited twice a year, and during our Christmas and summer visits I would sleep on a cot in her room. On one such visit I confided I was hurt that my girlfriend walked home from a dance with a boy while I had to trail behind. She listened and counseled me not to be jealous of my friend that my turn would come. I knew she loved me unconditionally. When she traveled up to Blue Point to see me, she revealed that she too had thought of religious life. I'm pretty confident the thought wasn't entertained for long, because Roxanna Jaxtheimer was a beauty and according to my mother, had seven proposals of marriage.

Holy Thursday, 1965 I wrote home that I didn't get the scholarship I had applied for. I also applied for a graduate assistantship in English. Later, Sister Joseph told me that I had gotten the assistantship. Everything was done with the suggestion and approval of Mother Vicar. I didn't begin the assistantship; however, and nothing more was said about it. If my mother hadn't saved my letters, I doubt I would have remembered it. But I'm sure at the time I would have been disappointed, and probably suppressed the resentment with an "All for Jesus."

Holy Thursday was a special day in the convent. We dressed in our Sunday best and attended Maundy Thursday services. Then we went to the refectory and had a delicious meal in silence- roast lamb and potatoes and vegetables served with wine, our version of the *Seder*.

I told my parents that I was observed by Dr. Bachman, a professor of English. I gave a poetry lesson on Edgar Allan Poe's " Eldorado" and "Annabel Lee." I was nervous and happy to get it over with. Mother General from Belgium was visiting Blue Point at the end of May. We had been postulants when she last came to visit us. The Vatican Council had recommended that religious orders take a fresh look at their customs and habits. So Mother Vicar had us go into New York City to get fitted for our new robes. I would be graduating from St. John's University on June 13, 1965, and soon after I would be taking final vows as an Ursuline of Tildonk.

My parents and my brother came to graduation on St. John's campus. I received my diploma and was officially a *Baccalaureatum in Artibus*. I had graduated *cum laude*. We had a nice dinner by ourselves at a restaurant. I returned to Blue Point to prepare for my final profession of vows. More prayers, more meditation and the requisite eight-day retreat of concentrated preparation took place. But I still battled doubts about my vocation, without however, the highflying emotional hysterics preceding my first profession. The changes in the administration of my world were far more dramatic. As Junior sisters we were not privy to the great changes coming soon. Mother Ursula would no longer be our Mother Superior and Vicar. She had recently celebrated her Golden Jubilee and she was being recalled to Belgium. Mother Philomena would become our new Mother Superior and Provincial.

Mother Ursula, Sr.Christine   Final Profession Blue Point, NY 1965

At the end of our retreat we were presented with the faults that our superiors thought we would need to work on for the rest of our lives. It was a performance review. And I thought I had failed dreadfully.

LsJC

> *In the spirit of Holy charity and out of Holy Obedience, the following remarks are made to Sister Mary Christine.*
>
> *Sister Mary Christine fails in Generosity by leaving difficult situations rather than making greater efforts to overcome them.*
>
> *Sister Mary Christine fails in Humility by being too sensitive. Sister is inclined to be self-centered instead of considering the feelings and happiness of others.*

Sister Mary Christine fails in Holy Obedience by being self-willed and independent but has made great efforts to receive corrections and be submissive.

Sister Mary Christine makes unnecessary remarks during the time of silence and speaks too loudly

On the reverse of this typed sheet of paper I wrote a response to the Blessed Mother:

LsJC

Dear Mother,

These are the faults seen in me by my Superior's before God. I accept it from your hands.

But I am bitterly ashamed of the picture of me.

It seems to be the antithesis of what a religious should be. But God's Holy Will be done.

Destroy in me all that would prevent His Will from being accomplished but as for the rest all belongs entirely to you.

Be my generosity and support in difficult situations, be my humility and focus my thoughts on you and on others.

Be my submission and take my will. Help me to listen to Jesus in my soul and teach me to speak softly.

I love you Mary, please help me.

———∽∽∽⊱———

Six years is a long time to ponder a decision. I can fault no one for my indecisiveness. I brushed aside the nagging doubts that roamed about in my head as temptations. Being a nun is God's will for me, I thought. And most of the time I convinced myself of it, but then the "what if's" would rear their tiresome heads. I was so deliriously happy after I took the veil as a novice, that common sense should have warned me that it could not last. And it didn't. Eventually, I experienced what could be called a dark night of the soul or in psychology-speak, a depression. Prayer became a torture. I did not feel God's love in anything I did. It was an excruciating time, but it eventually passed. Reportedly, Mother Teresa of Calcutta lived most of her life in such a state, doubting even the existence of God. This stoicism may eventually bring her sainthood in the Catholic Church, but at what cost. It saddens me to think of it.

However, we six made our profession of final vows with little fanfare. I remember the priest who gave the sermon said in a jocular fashion, something like, "well I guess you'll have a blast today, play some pool, right?" If only, Father. There was little rejoicing. A pall had fallen over Blue Point. The older sisters were concerned about the momentous changes coming when Mother Ursula would step down as Vicar and Mother Philomena would become the new Mother Superior. But as newly professed we were not confided in and our new status as professed was barely noted.

When my parents visited later in the summer I explained what I thought was happening. My father had more sympathy for Mother Vicar than I did. He was moving ever closer to retirement and he knew what it was like to get old and be passed over and moved out. Although once the Novice Mistress had asked, "Why does Reverend Mother like you?" The question irritated me. I never felt the recipient of any favors. Quite the contrary. When sisters traveled down to New Jersey, the Vicar could have suggested that I be dropped off for an afternoon visit at my parents. But she did not. When my beloved grandmother died, she could have suggested I go to the funeral. But she did not. And one evening when I had delivered something up to an ill sister in the professed wing of the convent, I unexpectedly crossed paths with Mother Vicar who was dressed in her nightclothes and returning to her room. She informed me that I had missed graduating *magna cum laude* by a fraction of a decimal point. I had disappointed her, I felt crushed, and later I felt angry.

There was a strained farewell of sorts in the library. Reverend Mother sat at the desk and we entered one by one and knelt by her side to say good-by. I knew I was supposed to say something nice. Although I felt that she was expecting more from me, I resisted. Every day when I left for St. John's, I knelt while she traced the sign of the cross on my forehead and said: "Off you go now." On this day, Mother Ursula made her last cross on my forehead. I simply said good-by and wished her well. I got up and walked out. Simple. Direct. Finis. Mean. Insufferable yet again.

I totally forgot what I had written just five years earlier in my Explanation of the Holy Rule, On the Duties of the Superior:

> *The position of a Superior is not an easy one. Not only has she the corporal welfare of the religious, the care of the house and many other material worries but she carries the burden of the spiritual advancement of each of the sisters...We must always respect our Superior as representing God and respect everything which is for her use. Some pious Jesuits raise their hats in passing the Superior's room. We should act in the same spirit.*

Mother Ursula's exceptional story should be more fully told.

—————

When I received my teaching assignment I was very excited. I was going to Our Lady of Grace in Howard Beach to teach fourth graders. Since I had had a happy summer there, I was looking to it because I'd also be with friends from novitiate days. The school was attached to the convent. So we could go from the second floor right into the school corridor. The community room was large and bright. I told my parents:

*I have a nice room on the third floor. What a view
at night. You can see the lights of the airport and it's
a beautiful sight. The beds are good – I go out like a
light. Mother Benignus said you could see the house
the next time. Grandma might like to see my classroom too. I'll have the bulletin boards done and the
room decorated.*

I felt my superior was intelligent, thoughtful, and fair. In all the
houses the superior was also the principal of the school. The school
was well run and the children were well behaved, and I had plenty of
time to prepare for classes. We rose early as usual, said our Office
in private, had meditation and Mass, rosary, breakfast and dishes.
We would go outside and lineup with our children and the school
day would begin. At lunch we walked back to the convent and sat
down to a dinner cooked by a hired woman. We had recreation,
prayers and then headed back to school. Many working mothers
would like those "hardships." In the afternoon we were free to go
to our rooms to lie down if we wanted to. We had charges that had
to be done as needed. Supper was fixed by us on a rotating basis.
We did the dishes and then went to Chapel. After that we had the
evening to talk, grade papers and prepare for classes in the community room. We were now allowed to read or study in our bedrooms with lights out at our own discretion. On Sundays after all
the Masses, we sat in the community room and counted the collection money, which took about an hour, and then we were free until
supper in the evening. The routines were fine and the workload
manageable. All in all, things were looking up.

The Ursulines acquired another estate. This time it was in Oys-
ter Bay, New York. It had been a summer place and had riding trails
and a hunter's cabin on it. One provision in the bequest stipulated
that it could never become a school. We were allowed to invite our
family out for a picnic on the grounds. So my parents drove up
with my Grandmother Bassler and picked me up at Howard Beach
and then we continued on to the estate. We walked the property
by foot. I was told it would take twenty minutes by horseback. The
tour of the house took fifteen minutes including the pool, rose gar-

den, patio with sundial, circular staircase and mirrored reception room. I had a nice time, but my parents were fuming over the news that my brother was moving into an apartment with another lawyer. Although the word "gay" was never spoken, my parents were afraid of what people would think. My grandmother and I thought their fuss was all nonsense.

September 27, 1965 I wrote:

> *This must be a quickie. It's 9:30 and I've just finished correcting about 4 sets of papers (58 each) My little peepers are closing. Boy, so much has happened. I survived the first fire drill.*

I know fire drills are necessary, but I hate them. By law they always have to be given in the first weeks of school. So you know they're coming. You just don't know when. The fire exits are posted and the children are taken out the assigned door so everybody knows where they are going. But this Principal did a very smart thing that, thank God, I've never seen duplicated. She randomly blocked a passageway, which of course could happen in a real fire. So you had to think on your feet and take another way. One time that meant that I took the students up on the roof and crossed to the far side and down. I will never get over that.

In the same letter I go on: *Next Monday the Pope arrives. We have been assigned area "I" by the road leading to the airport. The 6th, 7th, 8th graders will go. It'll be a holiday for me, hurrah!* Pope Paul VI was the first pope to visit New York City. On Monday, October 4, 1965 he was going to St. Patrick's Cathedral in Manhattan, to the Waldorf-Astoria to meet President Lyndon Johnson, to the United Nations, to the Vatican Pavilion to see the *Pieta,* and finally he was going to say Mass at Yankee Stadium. This was to take place in twenty-four hours. Far from being a holiday, it became an exciting marathon. We went on buses with the school children and lined them up to wait to see the Pontiff ride from Kennedy Airport in his "bubbletop" limo. We were standing a long time to wave and cheer like crazy as he went by. Then we went back to the convent and ate.

The next assembly was at Yankee Stadium. We got there early so we could get a good spot to see right at the fence albeit a long way from the dais. So again we stood for hours. It was a long day, but in the spirit of Walter Cronkite: I was there, October 4, 1965.

I sent an anniversary card to my parents who were celebrating their thirty-second wedding anniversary on October 23rd.

> *Well our coats came, mom. They are beautiful and they fit. Thursday after school we drove down to Gerty's in Jamaica and bought raincoats. They have a lining for winter that zips out and they were on sale. So we're all fixed up. We'll wear the raincoats to school and save our good coats for Sundays and holidays.*

I had good news to tell my Dad in his November birthday card.

> *Last night Mother told us of the latest changes. The eleven days home is increased to fourteen days including travel but it can be divided up during the year any way at all! All mail to anyone in-going and out-going is private. We seal our letters. There are more I'll tell you about when I see you...*

December 17th I wrote:

> *Are you as excited as I am? Christmas isn't even two weeks away. Time flies in school. This is a very busy time. It seems like yesterday since Thanksgiving when we went out to the "cove" and "romped." Sr. Walter and I impersonated Squanto and Samoset but we couldn't get many people to "play along." We also did some bike riding. When we got home we had our delicious turkey dinner. Sr. Emile and I took advantage of our holiday to practice. A Hot Time in the Old Town Tonight is cute. Sr. Emile loves Malaguena and she sends a big "Thank you." I have*

a page and a half of <u>Rustles of Spring</u> memorized
but I don't think I'll get too much more time to prac-
tice now. I've got a few good runs for the Steinway,
though. Give my love to my brother. I have a special
"surprise" for everyone – not much but we'll have a
good laugh over it. Til Xmas God love you.

After my Grandfather died, money was tight for my Grandmother Kerr; so mom sent her what money she earned teaching
piano lessons. Grandma kept a record and when she died, her
will stipulated that the money be returned to her daughter after
the house was sold. My mom used it to buy her beloved Steinway,
which I now cherish in my home.

—◦◦◦—

At Christmas I was going home for the first time in six years! I
cannot begin to explain what that meant to me. My Grandmother
Bassler and my Uncle Marvin Kerr both from Pennsylvania would
be there too. My parents drove up to Howard Beach to pick me up
because Sr. Emile was letting me borrow her accordion. My father
made an audiotape of Christmas Day that I still have. It was so
much fun. We were all trying to make each other happy because
we missed my Grandmother Roxy. My mother played the piano
in between getting dinner ready. My Grandmother B played her
favorite *Sweet By and By* on the piano. My Uncle played *Good Night
Irene* on the guitar that my parent's had given him for Christmas.
My dad played the trumpet and my brother with feigned patience
also played the piano and acted as our Master of Ceremonies. We
must have played *Oh When the Saints Come Marching In* at least
thirty times. My father and I also played the recorders for a baroque
touch.

I hadn't slept in my old room in six years and my mom had
it all fixed up. When it was time for bed, she shyly came into my
bedroom, to see me as her daughter without the habit she dreaded
so much. I took off my veil. See, it's just me. I also hadn't seen my
best friend, Joan now called Sr. Alan, in six years. I got a chance to

spend time with her while she was visiting her parents as well. It was a very emotional visit.

**Sr. Christine, RU and Sr. Alan, RSM
Held's living room Christmas 1965**

I wrote home January 2, 1966:

We had a nice Christmas week I enjoyed every minute of it. It hardly seems possible. We had a good "jam" session, boy, that will get funnier as time

goes on. I've sight read McDowell's To a Wild Rose,
Mom. Not too hard. Sr. Emile loves the accordion
books. Such a nice selection of pieces. We have a lot
of good times to look forward to and that's the nic-
est part of these changes...The nuns laughed when
they saw my bundles. Looked like three sisters were
returning, they said. Mother Benignus is sending all
the handmade items out to Blue Point. Would you
be interested in coming to the Fair the next time?

I just came up to my room to put on my loafers. Mom
they are beautiful and comfortable. My watchband
is really good looking. Many of the sisters have them
now. It's better than buying a new leather one every
year. Thank you, Mom for all the work and fixing up
etc. I know you love to do it for me but I appreciate
it just the same. You'll be able to take things a little
easier at Easter. Thanks Dad for the driving. I know
Grandma and Marv loved having Christmas with
us. At least we made it noisy for them, ha!

I hope and pray you'll have improvement with the
Doctor, Mom. Another seventeen-year-old boy died –
probably dope. All the mother could say was "I don't
have to worry about him anymore." That was her
only consolation...

I chose my words carefully when writing to my mother, and I'm
not sure why I included this tragic news in my letter, except that I
knew that my mother still missed me, and I was pointing out that
things could be far worse. I wasn't dead. I doubt it consoled her.

We continued to go to many, many funerals. Most of them were
for Vietnam soldiers who returned home in caskets. We would go
to the funeral home and say the rosary with the priest and extend
our condolences to the suffering families. I did it sincerely as an act
of charity, but on another level I was merely a detached observer.

Thankfully, I had no loved ones involved. Would the war never end, I wondered.

A month later:

> *Last Friday we went on retreat at the Cenacle Retreat House...It snowed so much we couldn't go back on Sunday. But we could use the time at home because report cards were due on Tuesday. I'm getting a sore throat right now feel tired out. I'll be looking forward to the Easter break...*

I was plagued with sore throats. When I was little, my mom and grandfather would take me to church on the Feast of St. Blaise, February 3rd. I would kneel down and the priest would hold crossed candles under my chin and pray: *Per intercessionem S. blasii liberet te Deus a mal gutteris et a quovis alio malo.* St. Blaise was a bishop in Armenia and was martyred around 300 A.D. He had saved a child choking on a fish bone. Unfortunately, it didn't help me. The letter continued:

> *Well, Grandma's rugs arrived. One came on Friday and the other today. They are really lovely. The sisters thought they were beautiful and they are. She picked such bright colors. It's hard to believe she'll be 90 in a few weeks. And surprise of all, Mother Benignus said "Would you like to keep one for your room, we need rugs?" but I think I'll ask Grandma to make one for me and send these two on to Blue Point for the fair. They look so pretty in the room because the walls are just a plain pale pink and so the rug stands out in all its glory – ha! Wasn't that thoughtful of Reverend Mother?*

It was pretty thoughtful of my mom and grandma too. Braided rugs are valued in no small part because of the labor involved. My mom would go to a used clothing store and buy wool coats. They had to be taken apart and washed. Then cut into strips. The strips were folded so that the edges didn't show and then braided. The braids would be formed in an oval or round shape and sewed into place. My mom also donated many of the handmade linens and things from my Grandmother Kerr's estate for the annual Fair that the community had to raise money. I, in the spirit of poverty, even gave away three porcelain dolls. My Grandmother Kerr had clothed these dolls in beautiful handmade dresses. I wish I had them back. And my Grandmother Bassler generously made new braided rugs for the event as well. I wrote to my father:

> *Sister Emile's grandfather died suddenly last week. She and her sister went to Connecticut for the funeral. I am glad we are able to go to our grandparent's funerals now. It's too bad the rules weren't changed sooner. It must be hard for the older sisters. They missed out on a lot of things that we are enjoying. But that's life I guess.*

> *When I wrote to my brother, it was right after Mother Philomena came for her visitation and I told him some news. I don't know if he said anything or not. Well dad guess what! I'm going for my masters in Physics. Would you believe it – the irony of life, ha! They need them in the new high school and we don't have enough sisters ready. I'll have at least 20 credits in undergraduate school before I ever start on the Masters. The work! But it should be interesting and (if I pass) fun. Experiments and all. Mother Vicar said it would be a challenge for me. This may change summer plans and it may not. I might start studying this summer but will definitely begin next Sept. And I'll be going to Fordham most likely. There is also a possibility I might be transferred out of Howard Beach, me thinks, to Connecticut. Since we're opening a new grammar school in Shippin Point in Connecticut and the new high school in Huntington, L.I.*

*many changes are necessary. Who said religious life
is dull or monotonous?*

*I'm reading a very interesting and well-written book
entitled <u>Martin Luther</u> by Todd. A lot of misunder-
standing and legends about Luther are cleared up.
It isn't written by a Catholic, I don't think. But he
tries not to be prejudiced one way or the other. As I
read it, it seems pretty fair analysis to me.*

Again I am excited that I will be sent for a Masters in Physics,
no less. I loved science and had given up all thought of pursuing
it. I wrote another long letter to my parents in February, 1966. It
shows what life was like for me once I had left Blue Point and was
living in the houses. It was not a life of drudgery. We worked hard
with our children but we had lots of fun too. Living close to the city
offered great opportunities for our students and for us. I was clearly
excited about all the changes that were taking place in the Church
and in the convent.

*I saw the movie Dr. Zhivago yesterday in the city 50th
and 8th avenue. It was being shown free for the nuns.
What a beautiful theater. We took the subway in
and at 9:15 there weren't any seats left. I sat on the
steps in the balcony (with a lot of others) the management apologized. They didn't expect so many. I
thought the movie was tremendous. I had read the
book this past summer. You would have laughed at
Sr. Walter and Sr. Domenica and me getting home
by ourselves on the subway. We didn't see the others
after the show. There were so many nuns. There are
even more changes in rules. Mother Vicar is going to
Belgium Easter week and more changes are expected
on her return. Please write or send homing pigeons
but let me know if you're coming or not.*

I went to Carnegie on Sunday. What a treat. We took eight children on the subway. No trouble. It was the Youth Symphony Orchestra. No one was older than twenty. The tickets were free. I loved every minute. Sr. Walter and I were chosen to be on the parish committee for ecumenical affairs here. Don't know anything about it yet but should be very interesting. The parish priest and seven laymen and women are also on it...

After I left the convent, I tried to run for a seat on the parish council but I didn't know enough people and so I didn't get it. My brother recently asked me what happened to those reforms of the Vatican II Council. One may well ask. They were quietly, systematically, and effectively put aside. But I cannot help thinking that if they had been truly implemented as designed, the plague-like pedophilia vermin might have been brought to light sooner and exterminated.

My brother was now engaged to Eileen Schilling. Their engagement party went well followed by the traditional "meet the parents" dinner at our house. My Mom was a wreck. She bought two new chairs so there would be adequate seating for the Schillings. I wasn't there, of course, but by all accounts the dinner was a success as well.

In May 1966 I wrote home:

I can hardly believe that May is here. Now I know why I was so tired. I must have been fighting a virus. Last Wednesday I was sick with a sore throat. One of my children won't be back to school until Monday. It's so easy to pick up a "bug." I feel better now. I'm taking my class and the other 4ᵗʰ grade teacher is taking her class to the Museum of Natural History and then to the Bronx Zoo on May 27ᵗʰ...

Child's sketch of Sr. Christine on a bus by C.P.

It was on this trip to the Bronx Zoo that one of my fourth graders drew my picture on the bus. It's a perfect likeness and I kept it in my prayer book all these years, only to find it when researching this memoir. I wish I knew the little girl's name. However, I will never forget walking my group of fourth graders through the baboon section when one of them said in a loud voice: "Sister, what is that?" I followed the line of his pointing finger and then turned as red as the baboon's bum. There were other adults in the same enclosure or my response would have been different – maybe. I didn't really know what "that" was but I figured it was sexual because of where it was. I tried distraction. "Look over here. This one is eating." I felt certain that the adults enjoyed some amusement at my embarrassment. Maybe, I'm more mature now, but I still feel uncomfortable looking at baboons.

Living close to St. John's University gave us many opportunities that we didn't have at Blue Point. I wrote home:

> *We went to a lecture last night at St. John's. Dr. Dietrich von Hildebrand gave a paper on Time and Timelessness. He is 70 and quite a personality. He fled Austria when Hitler came to power. He left his house and everything with only $100 in his pocket. He is a philosopher. It was very interesting. Keep well...*

Pope Pious XII called Dietrich von Hildebrand "the 20th century doctor of the Church." He was a professor at Fordham University from 1941 to 1960 when he retired. He continued to lecture and write until his death in 1977. So when I heard him lecture he was older than I thought, probably 77. He was a conservative and wrote a paper titled "The Case for the Latin Mass" in 1966. He didn't like the new liturgical changes and didn't have any good words to say about Teilhard de Chardin and his opinions about original sin either.

———◦◦◦———

This next period of my life is difficult to understand even for me. My brother once asked why when the rules were relaxing did I want to leave the convent and come home? It's a reasonable question, but I don't have an easy answer, even after all these years. Perhaps because while visits home were at first wonderful, they had a dark side. In my journal I wrote:

> *How upset I became after this last visit home has taught me a lot and I am determined to work at it as I would a fault...even though I've been separated from home for six years I'm still far too attached. How difficult Jesus. Help me to achieve independence of spirit and maturity of character that I must have if my dedication as a nun is to mean anything. Who knows how pure my motives were for entering. Maybe I was unconsciously trying to get away or satisfy other needs. Help me now to purify my dedication...If I can achieve emotional and psychological healthfulness it can only contribute to my spiritual health.*

I had cried so many lonely tears when I first entered the convent as a seventeen year old. I had struggled with my attachment to my family. I had missed them so much, the jokes, the laughter, even the fighting and feisty political discussions at the dinner table. I thought I had overcome my need for my family and replaced it with my need for God. Yet here I was a fully professed nun making visits home for the first time in six years and I felt such a longing to return. It was as if I hadn't confronted my attachment at all. How could I be a good nun if at the first real taste of home the pull to return was overwhelming?

I went home for my first vacation in six years in June. My parents took me to Williamsburg, Virginia. We had a wonderful time. The motel had a pool and my mother and I went swimming every day. My father fixed cool Tom Collins drinks for all of us when we got back from sightseeing. I, of course, wore my habit because we were supposed to; and there were many sisters at the historical site, so I didn't feel self-conscious. Later when we drove up through the Blue Ridge Mountains, we stopped at a restaurant to eat. When I walked in, every head turned to look at me and stare. I might as well have been in a burqa from the Middle East. Anyone else would have donned secular clothes for the duration of the vacation and owned up to it when she got back. My best friend told me that's exactly what she did. Not me. Black or white. Yes or No. You're supposed to or you're not supposed to. No shades of grey in my crayon box, and absolutely no common sense.

I wrote home afterwards:

> *I woke up this morning and for a split second didn't know where I was – Ha! I just want to thank you again for everything. The wonderful vacation and all those delicious meals. I really had a good time... We really did do an awful lot in nine days. I loved the boat Dad. It is a beauty. Now I know where you get your bruises, mom, some of them anyway. I think I got two or three just in "readying about." When I find out my new phone number at Stamford I'll let you know. Til then keep tacking – fair winds ahead.*

But fair winds were not ahead for me. I thought I got along fine with my superior during the school year, but after that I found it difficult to talk to her easily. I wrote in my journal:

> *This strangeness must communicate itself to others especially my Superior with whom I have absolutely no rapport...I am not praying. My meditations are a time of self-pity. I do not even feel comfortable with God. How can I see the truth and yet not fall into a delusion of "poor me" attitude. Persecution complex etc. I cannot reach holiness that way. Bitterness and discouragement are my greatest enemies and temptations. How can I escape them?*
>
> *At times a feeling of disgust for religious life and regrets that I ever tried it pass over me like they used to.*

I haven't experienced this since before final vows. I am afraid of this feeling and the concomitant desire to leave. Lord Jesus help me! If I do not believe at least in my vocation and in God's love for me there is nothing left...Sometimes I think I'm a crackpot and my desires for holiness only neurotic compensations for my inferiority complex. Dear Jesus I hope not... the only prayer I say with any attention is the Office which I still love.

I missed chanting the Office, I missed the richness of the liturgy, I missed the contemplative life of the motherhouse. I had really left the semi-cloistered life behind when I left Blue Point, and I was having a difficult time finding my way. I felt I had no one to confide in. At home my father was studying Celestial Navigation through a correspondence course, but I was the one in need of a navigator. My life was getting complex, and the seas were getting rough. And then I received the news that I was being transferred to a new school in September. I was going to St. Maurice's school and convent in Glenbrook, Connecticut to teach third graders. I would be facing a new Superior and Principal, a new curriculum, and a new house of sisters.

In September I went down to New Jersey for my brother's wedding. My new superior, Mother Evangelist, kindly gave me a small white Bible to give to the couple as a gift. I attended the wedding liturgy, but I was not permitted to attend the reception which would involve drinks and dancing. The rules did not permit it. I wasn't complaining, because two years earlier. I wouldn't even have been able to attend his wedding. The Schillings had a party back at their home after the wedding reception, but my parents didn't go because I had been home by myself since the wedding Mass. My brother and I had always been close, and I was happy for him and for my new sister-in-law, Eileen.

I had sixty third- graders in my class that year. They were good little kids and stayed in their seats. Thank God! They did whatever "Sister said." I was taking organ lessons and I played for services in the parish Church and took care of the children's choir. I also had one piano pupil after school. One evening a week I took a Calculus course at the University of Connecticut.

After Thanksgiving 1966, I wrote home:

We had a 9:00 Liturgy in the convent followed by a big breakfast. The sisters from Shippan came over. Mother Philomena is staying with us until Monday. We decided we needed a change so we called up some children and borrowed their bicycles. Boy, did we have a good time bike riding – in fact, I'm still a little saddle sore. Then we played a little basketball up in the schoolyard. At one-thirty we had hors d'oeuvres and Whiskey Sours in the living room. We were singing and having a grand time. I had two wooden spoons and was banging away on two little bongo drums. Anyway...the doorbell rang – see and I foolishly pulled back the curtain a speck and said, "It's the cops!" However since I had door duty on Thursdays I got up and opened the door. There before me stood two men in black. One said with a smile – "It's the cops." Then the alcoholic sodden wheels began to churn and I mumbled something about "May I take your coat and hat your Excellency?" For indeed it was the Bishop!!

He had been up to visit the Monsignor and hearing about the bicycle sisters decided to stop in. Well anyhow we gave him a seat and offered him a drink. But he took ginger ale!!! He said the other stuff spoiled it for him – party pooper. Well, Mother having had two herself began to entertain His Excellency with a few Irish jokes. Then we sang a round of Galway Bay. When they finally left we couldn't believe it. Well we had a delicious dinner – turkey and ham. Champagne and all the trimmings. Followed by polkas, Charleston's, waltzes and a few reels. All in all the day was a success and we enjoyed ourselves immensely.

These rare moments of frivolity were enjoyable, and I wanted to share them with my parents. However, I really wasn't feeling well. My wisdom teeth were impacted. I had had two out in the novitiate. Now I had another one taken out, but I still had a bottom one to go, and I wasn't looking forward to having that out.

In November I wrote:

> *Well this was a fast week. I'm watching "Larry W"*
> *(Lawrence Welk) right now. Nursing a tooth extrac-*
> *tion! The bottoms aint like the tops! There was a*
> *bone in the way of my wisdom tooth so that was tak-*
> *en care of first. He closed over the "hole" with two*
> *stitches. Ice is keeping the swelling down and I have*
> *pills for the pain so I guess I'll live.*

I had met a friendly young woman at UConn when I started my Calculus course. She gave me rides back and forth to school. She played the drums, which helped her to win the "Miss Stamford" title. She offered to play for my third graders and the sisters at the convent. She set up two drums and two cymbals in our little living room. The place rocked and everyone enjoyed her because she had such a nice personality. Once on the way home from school she stopped to show me her efficiency apartment. I had never seen a living space so small.

In December a group of us took the train into the city to enjoy the sights and sounds of Christmas. We wandered around in the 5th Avenue stores admiring the beautiful decorations, not at all enticed by the expensive items for sale. Actually I remember think- ing: even if I had the money, how would I choose a pocketbook from the hundreds on display? In addition to train fare, Mother Evange- list had generously given us lunch money and we went to Horn and Hardart. I picked out an inexpensive luncheon special. We were in high spirits as we waited for the cashier to ring us up. But some man who had observed this group of fresh-faced, happy nuns paid our bill. We were delighted and grateful, but I thought to myself if I had known beforehand I'd have chosen something more expensive and delectable. So much for Holy Poverty. In those days many people treated nuns in habits with deference, and business men often gave them special deals. Cab drivers were the exception.

I took the train and bus down to New Jersey for an impromptu visit with my parents. I wrote:

> *I don't have much luck with taxis. I got to the Port Authority at about 6:25. Anyway I didn't get a taxi. It's quite a game, the fleet footed, sharp eyed dwarves do OK but us Hobbits...I walked to 42nd street and took the bus down to Grand Central. I had no trouble and got the 7:05 train as scheduled. We had a lovely weekend. Thank you so much for the delicious dinner and enjoyable Saturday night concert – both surprises. To tell you the truth I felt a little twinge at leaving but it would be sadder if I was anxious to go, ha!*

My parents had tickets to hear Arthur Rubenstein in Newark. My Dad gave me his ticket so Mom and I could sit together. He was going to wait for us outside, but he was lucky and bought a ticket out on the sidewalk so he was able to sit at the back of the concert hall. I sat in awe listening to one of the greatest pianists of all times. I still have the Playbill.

January 21, 1967 I wrote:

> *Didn't expect to write this weekend but it's 9:30 and I'm not sleepy and I don't feel like doing anything especially studying so I'll just sit and chat awhile. Lord knows I have enough to do. We had the children's tests this week and so they have to be corrected and then all the marks have to be averaged and put on their report cards, ugh! I was planning on getting a lot done this weekend because we have Monday off. But I had a sore throat this weekend and it's*

finally culminated in a runny, drippy, sneezing mess.
I took a nap this afternoon. I had a surprise math
test on Monday evening. Oh boy! I didn't do so good
– 68. Our final is this coming Wednesday 5:30-7:30.
I haven't gotten down to studying that much either!
I had a nice chat with Bill and Eileen. I think it was
Saturday. I asked how she was feeling and she said,
"Oh, you know?" I said "yes" Mom told me – sorry
Mom if I let the cat out of the bag. I figured by this
time if they didn't tell me, they would have expected
you to tell me. Oh well. Nighty-night.
P.S. I took my children to the museum today

My mom had told me that Bill and Eileen were expecting a baby, but I was supposed to feign ignorance until they told me themselves, however I flubbed it. I flubbed the calculus course too. This was the first bad grade I had received in college. I was finally working a schedule that earlier groups of sisters had experienced; that is, teaching all day, taking care of chores in the house, and going to school at night. I found that I didn't do so well under those circumstances.

Despite the cheery letters I wrote home, I found living community life to be extremely difficult. I felt the Superior indulged some of the older sisters by overlooking their quirks and oddities. The Rule of St. Augustine mentions choir sisters and lay-sisters. Monasteries in the Middle Ages had basically two classes of sisters: educated women from wealthy backgrounds and others who could not read and thus couldn't pray the psalter in choir. The latter tended to the mundane duties of a convent. The Vatican Council tried to eliminate such archaic distinctions and it was not something that was ever discussed. However, at this house, I observed two sisters whose behavior I thought quite odd. One in fact, seemed to be a willing servant of the other. I didn't understand it and I didn't like it, or the sister who seemed to boss the other one around.

I presumed that they had mental problems, but I still found the behavior intensely irritating. Our convent was a small cape and we were on top of each other. One weekend my parents drove up to see me, a nice table was set in the living room for us to be served by the bossy sister mentioned above. So I told my parents as soon as they entered the door that I had to get out of the house. They could see how upset I was, and we took a drive.

I wrote home afterwards: *I feel like the goose at the end of the wild goose chase! I'm sorry you made such a long trip for such a short visit but I did appreciate it.*

Looking back it seems that this incident would have gotten back to the Superior. However she did not speak to me about my strange behavior. Perhaps because it would have given me an opportunity to discuss what bothered me, a can of worms not to be opened. So I'm as much in the dark now, as I was then. Except that a friend told me that she too witnessed the same dynamic in another convent. But my real problem was that I didn't have anyone to confide in. I needed a *gumba*. I needed help, and I didn't know who or how to ask for it.

Of course some sisters would confide in their confessor, but I hadn't had much success in the confessional. We had a retreat day during which I enjoyed the talks by Fr. Cuszak because so many relevant issues were brought to light. I probably thought too much about them, but I was trying to get a handle on how to actually live the religious life out in the houses. I found a conflict between being honest and straightforward and the need to empathize. I found a conflict between the need to be honest and the requirement to be loyal to the community.

I wrote in my journal:

> *Also nine times out of ten my honesty is stifled by silence for the sake of "peace" not rocking the boat, keeping irritation to the minimum avoiding argumentation which makes me nervous...We are not honest about the difficult people we live with either... Rank is still with us in a big way. Also importance of opinion varies from what grade you teach. Finally –*

this love and understanding bit is fine only when it's mutual.

Most people deal with the myriad personnel challenges that arise in the workplace, but they don't then go home and sit down with their boss and co-workers every night. But that is exactly what I did. If I experienced a problem with a sister at school, I would be sitting down to eat dinner with her in the evening. If I made a suggestion during recreation that we shouldn't sell milk at such and such a time during morning class; for example, the Principal could turn Superior in an instant, and deflect the criticism or suggestion by reminding me about an unrelated mistake I'd made in the house. I would even feel tense at the dinner table if two other sisters were testy over something that happened in school that didn't involve me at all.

During a retreat in 1967, I wrote in my journal:

> *It does not matter what I do – but what I am. I have renewed the determination to return to my ideals of charity and obedience. Particularly in the area of complaining to others. Most of the good of my "acts" of virtue are lost by this. And I've made no attempt to keep it in check. Help me to supernaturalize the tiny everyday humiliations and difficulties in school and at home. If I do not really believe you are present in the circumstances of everyday then I will never find You. And I'm living an impossibility. Increase my faith dear God. I feel or sense that I am in a period of waiting. Both in my prayer life and in my religious life. I hope I am ready for what lies ahead...*

When I was teaching and studying and going about my day, I did not dwell on these thoughts. My days were busy and I generally enjoyed them, but during times of quiet and meditation I would have time to think. Then I would begin to question what I was doing with my life. I would wonder if I would be able to sustain the effort for the years to come.

I wrote home in January 1967 that the pastor had died.

I am relieved that the funeral is over. I was tense worrying about the altar boys and the whole thing in general. The funeral service was beautiful. There were about one hundred priests and sisters present. After the Mass on Monday we drove up to the cemetery in Waterbury. We passed some of the places we had passed on Sunday and you wouldn't believe the difference in one day. From Spring to Winter! I got a 93 on the final exam but a B for the course. It wouldn't have killed him to drop the 68 quiz mark but he didn't so...at least I know I ended up with a pretty good grasp of it.

In fact, the professor was a sweet heart. He knew that if the young men sitting before him flunked out of college, they would have to report for the draft and end up in Vietnam. Yes, it was grade inflation, but he did his best to keep them out of harm's way.

After the pastor's funeral I wrote in my journal:

Snowfall
Death pall
Cold silent monotonous flakes
Softly smothering
Life
Changed but not taken away
The Rising Son
The Melting snow
Promising
Springtime

Mother Philomena made her visitation. When I went in to see her I had two things to unburden. The first had to do with an article I had been asked to write for an in-house publication. I think it was about St. Angela. Three paragraphs had been changed completely without anyone discussing it with me. This really "got my goat" as my grandmother would say. It burned me and touched the very core of my ego. I told my journal:

> *I was furious and angry to tears. I'm sorry I missed a real opportunity to suffer silently for you. With your help I'll keep my lips closed unless to mention it to Mother Vicar. Objectively, I think it's wrong. But subjectively, where is my humility?*

I found the courage to present the hurt to Mother Philomena and then I found peace. The second issue had to do with my health. I was constantly tired and not feeling well. Mother arranged for me to see a doctor for which I was grateful.

—◦◦◦—

But I was coming undone. My journal entry April 22, 1967 reads:

> *Spent most of the day in bed. Went to the doctor – swollen glands, tonsils infected. I feel tired and worn out. I worked hard all week. Vocation exhibit and talks. I enjoyed talking to the girls although I was nervous thinking about it. Somehow in explaining my life to others it makes more sense to me. The week has been too much for me though. Most days I haven't been able to get my prayers in or am too tired to say them. The most discouraging thing is the lack of help, support or encouragement (or sympathy or even concern over my health) of Mother Evangelist. Yet somehow it doesn't hurt much or else I'm just too tired to care anymore. But it is exasperating and frustrating. I feel she has it in for me in little ways – jealous perhaps, I don't know. I have tried to be cooperative. You are very near me Jesus and it is your grace supporting me. All for thee. Purify me of*

self-love. Help me to accept these petty humiliations
for love of You. Unite me to Thyself.

The year before, I had done something extremely lame, but I
didn't comprehend its impact until many years later. It was my first
year teaching. I had a class of sixty fourth- graders. I had a little boy
who I thought was very immature for his age and who would ben-
efit by being kept back a year. Amazingly, my Principal and superior, Mother Benignus accepted my decision to retain him. I say
amazingly, because Mother Evangelist and the Provincial, Mother
Philomena, were biological sisters and were the little boy's aunts.
Mother Benignus was their cousin. I was not aware of this interfa-
milial relationship at the time. However, I can only shake my head
in disbelief at my extreme naiveté and hubris. I heard later that the
little boy was sent to school in Ireland rather than be kept back in
the states. If Mother Evangelist didn't cozy up to me, who could
blame her? I was smug beyond belief and didn't even know it. I was
beyond insufferable at this point.

In an April 30th journal entry, I am feeling pretty sorry for
myself.

Not much sunshine now. Got through April and the
vocation exhibit and talks. Working on glee club
now – next week. Went to the doctor's – sinus and
throat infected – tonsils have to come out. They've
been diseased for years, he said. Monday I had an
excruciating headache – sick to my stomach even.
But I taught all day, gave a piano lesson, religious
instruction and even went to college that night. God
alone knows what it cost me. It is hard to suffer
without sympathy. I'm too tired to pray and I've
been negligent.

I feel so stupid. I don't want to go to the hospital. Two
days and a week's rest. This will interfere with sum-
mer school. I feel like crying and giving up. I wish I
could go home this summer for a month's rest. I don't

think, speak or act spiritually. There is no mortifica-
tion except the effort to accept the sufferings and work
of each day. But I feel numb spiritually

I had an attic room in this cape and I loved it. I was allowed to use Grandma B's braided rug and I had it beside my bed. It was a private oasis. Sometime during early spring, Mother Evangelist received a packet of surveys. She gave them out. I sat in my bed in my third floor hide-a-way and took the time to thoughtfully answer the rather long survey. It was prepared by the Leadership Conference of Women Religious. I suspect it was an outgrowth of discussions during the now closed Vatican Council II. I pondered one question in particular: Would you encourage a young woman to enter the convent? I answered, No. Then I thought if I would not encourage another, why was I still a nun?

I saw a doctor who said I needed to have my infected tonsils taken out. This would require an overnight in the hospital. I was very upset because it would be done when school was out; and therefore, it would change my summer plans. I loved taking classes and I loved going to St. John's. So I was terribly disappointed. But what really bothered me was that I would be in the house all summer. I wouldn't be teaching; so I would be spending a great deal of time with some sisters I could barely tolerate. I nearly had a total melt down. I told Mother Philomena I wanted to leave the convent. The where and when of the following events elude me, but I was taken to see a Jesuit. I had cried myself out the night before and resisted his efforts to elicit more tears. I have never liked manipulation. I told him I didn't believe in God or religious life. When I went back to my convent, I was given tranquilizers. It took tremendous effort to finish grades and report cards. I remember crying uncontrollably. Later I thought, if I have to take tranquilizers to live in the convent, then it simply couldn't be the life for me. I was like the poor, baby, blowfish I had toyed with at the bay. In or out; live or die. If someone didn't throw me back into the sea, I would suffocate and die.

On July 28, 1967 I became an aunt for the first time. I was allowed to travel to New Jersey for the christening, to visit with family, and to meet my niece, Julia. Holding this beautiful baby in my arms made concrete my former theoretical musings over the vow. I knew for a certainty that this good was far, far better than its opposite.

Four Generations of Basslers
First row: Grandma B, Eileen holding Julia, Bill
Back row: Mom, Dad, Sr.Christine

In August, I wrote in my journal:

Well, Lord this has been quite a summer. But I have learned a lot and suffered much. It is quite possible to leave the convent in good faith. How narrowminded are most nuns' comments about ex-nuns. I will never even pretend to judge those who go or those who stay.

*The whole affair has been deeply humiliating to me.
I cannot help wondering if God expects community
living from one with a temperament such as mine.
It really seems impossible. But I must hang on to
the belief that I am doing God's Will and the suffering will be beneficial to souls-somehow. It is difficult
however when even a priest will tell you that it isn't
a temptation. Well then what is it?*

*So I am left alone. I knew better than to unburden
myself to the superior. It only increases the pain. I
feel so dumb and stupid. Lord will there never be a
let up. I've come the closest to a nervous breakdown
as I've ever come. But somehow You have been near
not like the other times.*

*I have no defenses against people. I feel like a huge
sensitive and open sore that will not heal over – no
crust. Can I make it Lord without turning to bitter-
ness and resentment as my shield? Only your grace
and strength can do it Jesus. Please help me. Dear
Mother of God be my support.*

I do not remember who the priest was who told me not to see
my desires to leave as temptations, but I probably owe him my life.
Also he did not tell me I was tied to my mother's apron strings as
the novitiate confessor had done. Stronger than apron strings were
the psychological ties I had to my belief that God wanted me to be
a nun. For more than nine years I had seen myself as being called
by God to be a nun. So after a lifetime of trying to do God's Will in
every aspect of my waking day, I had to learn to tell God that I didn't
want to do his will. I also had to admit to myself that my childhood
dreams of sanctity were just that – wishful thinking. I wasn't going
to be Thérèse of Lisieux or Bernadette of Lourdes or even Mother
Teresa of Calcutta. I had to turn myself upside down and inside out.
I had spent most of my life cultivating the habit of God, and now I
would have to remove that habit if I were to be whole let alone happy.

The next year, 1968, I was transferred again. That made two states, three cities, three convents, three Principals / Superiors, three schools, three different grades and curriculum in three years. This would have challenged the most stable, well-balanced nun, and I was neither. If these constant changes in assignments were a test then I failed. But if they were a way of telling the volunteer "please leave" then I would oblige.

This time I was assigned to teach seventh grade at the Nativity of the Blessed Mother in Ozone Park. I liked the Superior, Sr. Gabriele, who had been an assistant Novice Mistress at Blue Point. My friend, Sr. Ruth Henry who had been my mentor in the novitiate, was there. And I was teaching 7th grade with two friends, Sr. Alice and Sr. Robert. Our classrooms were in a school annex about two blocks from the school. We worked together very well and had fun in the process. We taught American History as a team and held a Continental Congress with mock elections among the three classes. We actually took all of our students to Philadelphia for the day - we left before sunup and came home after nightfall. The students saw all the important sights including the Liberty Bell and the Museum of Science. What a great day for all of us! My ability to compartmentalize allowed me to thoroughly enjoy the day while in another part of my psyche I was moving closer and closer to leaving the convent.

During our free time on Sunday afternoons, Sr. Alice and I would have mini-adventures. She taught me the subway system, so I was able to get myself to Port Authority and visit home without asking my parents to drive me back and forth. One time we visited her mother. Another time we went to the Brooklyn Museum, a marvelous place that I haven't had the good fortune to visit again. I appreciated the companionship and the distraction of the outings. Sr. Ruth Henry tried to get me involved in good works. I visited a family in Spanish Harlem with her. Another time we went door to door encouraging families to vote against the so-called "Blaine Amendment" in New York State by voting for a new constitution which would allow some state funding to Catholic schools. Blaine

(1830-1893) attempted to change the U. S. Constitution and failed but his idea succeeded in all but eleven state legislatures. At this time another attempt to take it off the New York books was being made. I'd protest to my friend that I was too shy, but once inside the door I surprised her because I exhibited no reluctance to speak whatsoever. Notwithstanding our political efforts, the New York constitution held firm and state taxes would not be used to fund religious schools.

Once when I was in the schoolyard saying my rosary, a young curate, struck up a conversation. He often drove a few of us to the never ending funerals of Vietnam casualties. He had a great sense of humor. For some reason he told me that I was earning $900 a year. It didn't matter to me because I never saw it, and I didn't have to worry about money at all. Some of that money had to be sent to the Motherhouse to support the sisters and novices and Juniors going to St. John's University and the rest had to be used to support the house. Depending on the wealth of the parish, some pastors were more generous than others. The sisters were literally working for loose change. I admire the ingenuity of the house superiors to make it all work.

On November 27, 1967 after a trip home I wrote:

> *Thanks for driving me up. I appreciated it. I was awfully tired this weekend and was glad to get back early. Did you watch David Suskind from 8:00-9:15. I thought the priest and "former" priests spoke very well. I watched Anne Frank mom did you? It certainly is moving.*

> *Everybody seemed tired and in a "bad" mood today including me. Didn't feel much like teaching.*

> *December is going to fly by. The choirgirls were asked to sing for Midnight Mass on Christmas. So we'll have to buckle down to work. We're also singing at the PTA meeting Monday the 4th. Thanks again for the boots. They are beautiful and warm.*

I loved working with the children's choir. I can still see the candlelight procession with the Bambino around the church at Christmas Eve and my sweet little girls singing *Tu Scendi Dalle Stelle*. On a day-to-day basis things were not that bad. But the handwriting was on the wall. I had been sent to study psychology by my community, but when I gave an opinion about a convent practice that I thought was incompatible with good mental health, I got shot down. It was never going to get any better for me. I didn't know how to translate religious goals into the practical realities of living day to day in a community. It finally dawned on me that I would never be able to live this way for the rest of my life. The ideal and the real were opposite sides of the coin for me. If I were eventually going to leave, then it would be better to do it sooner rather than later, I reasoned. My classes were going well. I got on well with my house Superior. I finally felt physically well. This time, when I again told Mother Philomena that I wanted to leave, I had the emotional and physical strength to follow it through. I don't remember her saying anything to me; although, surely she did. I don't remember even trying to explain to her why I wanted to leave the convent. There was another visit to a priest, maybe another psychiatrist, but I don't remember. I do remember no tranquilizers were given this time. To her credit and my great relief, Mother Philomena, accepted my decision, and I was told I could write to the Bishop. I began to breathe more easily.

——⟨⟩⟨⟩⟨⟩——

In January, I met my parents at the Boat Show in New York City and told them that I was going to leave the convent. I hadn't really given them any warning except for the strange way I acted when they visited me in Connecticut the year before. Certainly my letters home reveal little of my inner turmoil. So it couldn't have been easy for them. They thought I was settled. The rhythm of their lives no longer revolved around me. They must have been concerned about how this was going to affect their relationship. Maybe they were concerned about what the Catholic neighbors or relatives would say.

I am guessing because we never had a discussion about any of these issues.

On February 17, 1968 I wrote to them:

What an enjoyable day we had. Thanks for the delicious lunch. I'm getting anxious about sailing this summer, Dad.

I can't tell you how relieved I feel about the whole thing and how thankful I am to have such understanding parents. I know this is for the best and that everything will work out. I have put a great deal of thought and prayer into it and for once I feel God is on my side. I don't really feel the past nine years have been a waste either. I have learned a lot and have grown up too. I am at peace with myself. The convent can take care of its own problems without me.

But I do ask you to pray for me these next few months. It will be nerve wracking and I only hope they Let me go peaceably without a big to do. They could put me through the mill. However, we'll take each day as it comes. I feel happy about it already...keep your eyes out for summer tutoring jobs. They're usually good paying too. Well, I have 150 history tests to correct. Take it easy and thanks again for everything.

When I told Mother Philomena about my plans, she did want me to wait until the end of the school year to be released from my vows. But I didn't want to, and I assured her that I would finish my teaching duties and not leave them in the lurch. So in March, I wrote a letter to the Bishop of Rockville Center asking to be dispensed from my vows. Basically, pleading irreconcilable differences. A no fault divorce, if you will. They were simple vows, and he had the authority to do it without Rome's approval. I was only a sister and not a nun.

April 4, 1968, Martin Luther King, Jr. was assassinated. Again we mourned with the nation. We sat and watched the chaos of grief on TV. It was the first time I had ever witnessed the funeral and burial rites of an African- American, and I was deeply touched. The 60's had happened and I had watched from the sidelines. Many Roman Catholic Sisters had participated in voter registration and the Civil Rights Movement. But I hadn't. My great-grandfather, Pastor Bassler, would have been disappointed in me. He kept a Journal in 1841 while he traveled into Virginia from Gettysburg to meet Lutheran communities in preparation for his consecration as a man of God. He writes:

> *A colored man, who is married to one of Mr. K's colored women, is owned by some man across the mountain, who inherited him from his parents. When they died they requested that he might be free which the son has most shamefully neglected to do. This colored man has now been hired out by his young master for a number of years and being an intelligent and smart man has earned for him about $1,200. Now the master is in want of money and wishes to sell the poor slave unless he can redeem himself, but to make his case desperate, if possible, he demands $1,200 more for his release. It needs no comment; it speaks for itself.*

And having the right to vote, to sit at the front of a bus or the front of a restaurant, to go to the school you choose, or to drink from a water fountain, also speaks for itself. At the senseless murder of Reverend King, riots broke out across the country even in Red Bank, New Jersey my hometown.

I went on a retreat before Easter with the rest of the sisters as I had done for eight years. I found this retreat comforting. The relief of finally deciding to leave the convent is evident in a poem I wrote. The depression is gone and a new life beckons. Spring promises renewal. I wrote about the flowering of a common roadside shrub.

Forsythia
You mock me
Flaunting hope in each lacy golden bough
Forgetting winter's barrenness
Unmindful of the summer's heat
Present glory of yellowness
You live in the Now!

Which of course is what I was trying to do - live in the now. Since I was no longer a member of the community there was some "shunning." I remember waiting alone at a state park because I couldn't do whatever the rest were doing. I had already been dispensed from my vows, and was therefore no longer a sister but a lay-woman, even though I still felt like Sister Christine. I could now sympathize with those who suffer from shunning of any kind, but I knew it would be short lived, and it wasn't done out of malice. It was my choice to revoke my vows earlier than later.

I wrote letters to my friends explaining my decision to leave the convent. I remember writing to my former Novice Mistress, Mother Genevieve, telling her that I hoped to continue to be a credit to her. The news spread to my high school history teacher and Forensics moderator, Sr. Vincent. She was my secret *gumba*. She stopped by the Nativity convent when she was visiting family in the area, and offered me a job at Red Bank Catholic High School. I so appreciated her concern and help, but politely refused. I had been in the Catholic system since I was six. I thought I needed a change. I mailed out numerous applications to public schools in a hundred mile radius and didn't get one call for an interview. I never even thought to approach St. John's about the assistantship position I had been granted three years earlier. I never even knew why I wasn't permitted to pursue it. I didn't get any responses or interviews from my query letters. I realized later that my college transcript from St. John's had my name as Sister Mary Christine Bassler, R.U. The public schools weren't looking for ex-nuns. It was my brother who secured an interview for me to teach at a public middle school in Red Bank.

When I went home after Easter, my mom and I went shopping for my get-a-way dress. I had already begun to let my hair grow. My Dad drove up to the convent to take my trunk home where I had packed my prayer books, journal, Holy Rule and my hand written Explanation of the Holy Rule that have provided along with the letters home, the backbone of this memoir. My dad and I thought the house was empty, and the sisters all out at Blue Point. The handle broke and the trunk bumped noisily down the stairs in the dead-quiet convent. My dad and I could hardly contain our nervous giggles. However, there was one lone nun in the house, Sr. Charles. She heard it all and made a humorous remark about it later.

I was told I wouldn't teach the last three days of school. If they thought I would have made a scene in front of my students, they really didn't know me at all. The night before I left, my kind friends, Sr. Alice and Sr. Robert, put my hair up in curlers. There were no formal good-byes. They had to teach the next day.

For the first time in nine years, I got up out of bed and didn't put on my habit with a kiss, but instead pulled a secular dress over my head. I think it was the ugly, little brown check number. I met the Superior and walked out the door. We got into the car and she drove me to the subway station. We simply said good-by. Sr. Gabrielle was a good superior and I liked her; I felt bad that my leaving happened on her watch, so to speak.

I got out of the car with my small suitcase, closed the car door and walked down the stairs to the subway. I was no longer #55, Sister Mary Christine, R.U. but once again Susan Ann Bassler. When the subway doors closed, I might as well have been teleported through a time warp from the Starship Enterprise. Where had I been? Where was I going?

ACKNOWLEDGEMENTS

Many thanks to Ruth Townsend Story, editor, mentor and shepherd of this project. Dorothy Balko, Beth Benjamin, Jean Cash, Roseann DalPra, Wilma DeGregorio, Joan Held Fitzgerald, Georgiana Gallagher, Florence Gandel, Elizabeth Jannuzzi, June Miles, Margaret Pickford, Richard S. Pickford,Jr., Phyllis Riddle, Susan Riley, Patricia Rotelli, Barbara Twigg. Also thanks to the two memoir writing classes at Osher Lifelong Learning Institute, University of Southern Maine given by Ruth Townsend Story and Norm Abelson; the Portland Public Library, Maine; the John S. Ketchum Library, University of New England.

Thanks to former Ursulines and current Ursulines who were generous with their time but wish to remain anonymous.

Special thanks to my son Richard Pickford III for his encouragement and computer help.

Gratitude to my brother, Honorable William G. Bassler, for his continued support.

Posthumous thanks to my mother, Ethel Kerr Bassler for the foresight to save my letters home and to my father, Sherman G. Bassler for the patience to photograph and chronicle the events of my life.

THE AUTHOR

Susan Bassler Pickford is a teacher and writer. She entered the convent at 17 and became an Ursuline of Tildonk. At 26 she left and returned home where she taught at Red Bank Catholic High School for four years and earned a MAT at Monmouth College. She married and moved to Chelmsford, Massachusetts where she raised two boys while continuing to teach at Keith Catholic High School now Lowell Catholic. She earned a MEd in English as a Second Language from UMass-Lowell and a Certificate of Advanced Study at Harvard and taught in the Lowell Public Schools until she retired. The family moved to the Portland area in Maine. Susan has taught at the University of New England as an adjunct faculty member since 2001. Her stories for children and plays for middle school students can be found on Amazon.com.

**Standing: Richard III, Richard, Jr. John Sherman
Sitting: Susan and Lisa holding Lucy Jane**

24725155R00087

Made in the USA
Middletown, DE
04 October 2015